In Praise of Single Women Over 40

The World Is Your Stage
Stand Front & Center

MICHELLE MENDOZA

Published by Aniel Publishing Inc., 2014

ISBN: 978-0-692-34436-1 (paperback)
          978-0-692-34965-6 (ebook)

http://www.inpraiseofsinglewomenover40.com
http://www.overview40.com
http://www.facebook.com/inpraiseofsinglewomenover40

Cover Photography by Abigail Marie, Nonpareil Photography
Cover & Interior Design by Carolyn Sheltraw
Book Editing by Maria Gonzalez

Printed in the United States Of America

Special Acknowledgments

To my parents, Ella & Aeneas, thank you for all of your support over the years. And, a special thank you to my mum who taught me never to give up on my dreams and always encouraged me to keep trying even when I hit roadblocks or encountered disappointments and setbacks.

And, whose strength and character inspires me through all the years you have fought and suffered with Systemic Lupus. To my dad, Benny, I will always love you.

Thank you Pete Masterson for sharing all of your invaluable resources with me and for your guidance in the publishing world.

Special thanks to Mark DiGennaro and your family. You have been a big part of my life as my partner, band mate and friend. I enjoyed being a part of all of your lives and the beautiful memories we shared at the Jersey shore! Keep the faith and keep on rockin'!

Thank you Loan Rae for your beautiful spirit, friendship and selflessness and for always remembering me in your prayers.

Thank you Tracy D. for making all of us laugh, for not being afraid to be yourself and not worrying about what others think of you.

Thank you Carolyn Sheltraw for an amazing book cover and design. I appreciate your quick replies and your professionalism. I have long been a fan of you work and am honored to have you work on my book.

~In Memory of
Augustine DiGennaro~

What a liberating experience to be able to write without restrictions and guidelines...utilizing one's freedom of speech. The ability to speak your truth and relay it in your own words...in your own way...an original. Some may love it...others may hate it and still others may not truly understand where you are coming from. And, yet others may criticize...looking for faults. But one cannot deny... that once pen hits paper something magical starts to happen...the writing takes on a life of it's own...and goes in an unexpected direction... and before you know it...you have an entire body of work that becomes the book that's found by just the right person...at the right time...because the words written on those pages have the power to inspire and even change a person's life. For those who love to read... you understand what a gift a book can truly be.

M.

Table of Contents

Part II – New Beginnings

Introduction

The Challenges Of Being A Single Woman Over 40

As single women in our forties, we face many challenges. Some of you may have gone through a recent divorce and spent the last twenty years raising a family. Others may be widowed or recently ended a long-term relationship with the person you thought you were going to marry. And, there are those of you who are married but feeling neglected and alone.

Our generation is bombarded with all kinds of grim stories about how difficult it will be to find somebody else at this stage of our lives. Not only that, we may suddenly find ourselves competing with women in their twenties, young enough to be our daughters, for men in our own age group.

Being single is now considered detrimental to our health and overall sense of wellbeing. A recent survey conducted by the Women's Health Center stated, "besides a possible boost in your standard of living, a joint household can mean less financial stress and better health." Even the Center For Disease Control & Prevention stated, "compared to singles, married people are less likely to smoke, drink heavily or use illegal drugs."

As singles we supposedly take less care of ourselves, we don't eat well, engage in more risky sexual behaviors and tend to smoke and drink more because we hang out at bars more picking up one night stands.

And, we are more likely to become crime victims according to the National Archive of Criminal Justice Data's Crime Victimization Survey. Having a partner should shield up from dangerous experiences. And, our partnerships should be the basis of our happiness and success in life.

But, those of us who have just gotten out of a toxic relationship know this is not true. And, if we put our faith in these reports, we will become the helpless, vulnerable, sex crazed, drunken, drug addicts who aren't capable of taking care of ourselves or functioning properly in society as these reports are implying.

Yet, it's not our single status that should have us worried. Staying in a physically, emotionally or mentally abusive relationship can cause more harm than being single.

Warning: A toxic relationship may cause you to behave in ways that make you look and act like a crazy person. You may also suffer from low self-esteem, upset stomach, sleeplessness, fatigue, depression, lack of appetite or over eating, stomach ulcers, headaches, multiple personality syndrome, rage and or anger and suffer emotional and mental abuse.

You may have gained weight from being depressed or if you are like me, lost weight because eating was not enjoyable. Your skin may look dry and haggard, broken out with acne caused by stress and gray hair appearing, as if overnight, aging you by a few years.

Fear may have kept some of you in toxic relationships longer than you should have and you may suddenly be lacking in self confidence and feel lost and defeated. Being in a relationship can be the greatest feeling in the world when the relationship is a healthy one.

You have less financial stress if you're splitting the finances and someone to look after you should you become sick. You have someone to share your life with and someone to hold and love you.

But, when the relationship takes a turn for the worst and there is no way to salvage it your mind is going in a hundred different directions trying to figure out what to do next. And, if you were like me that gave up everything for your relationship you may be nervous at the thought of having to start completely over. Will you be able to afford your own rent? Will you have to get a second job to help ends meet? And, will you ever meet anyone else?

It is a daunting task when the relationship has ended and you find yourself not only suddenly single in your forties but wondering how you are going to cope mentally and emotionally with starting over. And, in the back of your mind thinking about how difficult it may be to find someone normal and decent at this stage of your life.

I can tell you from first hand experience, you are not alone on this journey. I spent the last two and a half years with someone I met online that I gave up my entire life for that I had worked so hard to establish and by the end of the relationship was living near the poverty level.

Although, I was married in my early twenties, it only lasted four years before I ended it. I was young and inexperienced and was married to an extremely controlling husband from the Middle East who threatened to kill me if I left him.

I had a friend who helped me move out while he was on a business trip and literally had to go into hiding for a while, change my phone number and switching jobs so he would stop harassing and threatening to kill both me and the close girl-friend who helped me escape.

My next serious relationship came two years later when I was 27 years old. I stayed in that relationship for thirteen years before deciding, with mixed emotions, that it was time to end the relationship I had become so comfortable with. Although, I could have married Mark I chose not to because I had fallen out of love with him and decided we would make better friends.

So, when my last relationship came about I thought I had found a stable man who also happened to be a single dad with two children and owned his own business. The problem was he lived in the Midwest and I lived in Florida but we made it work until he convinced me to give up everything and move to the Midwest with him.

By the time I met Chris I was already in my early forties and didn't give it a second thought that I would have any problems finding someone else at my age. I was so happy to be in another relationship after a two year dry spell that I ignored all the warning signs that clearly showed me that this was not the right person for me.

Within seven months of dating him, I gave up my career job that I loved and paid me incredibly well and a beautiful condo in a high-rise building overlooking the intracoastal and Palm Beach.

Against my better judgement I relocated to the frigid Midwest to play housewife and part-time mother to an emotionally troubled preteen daughter and teenage son. Although I adored them, as time went on I realized I didn't have the parenting skills necessary to cope with children from a divorced home who were still young and trying to adjust to their parents no longer being married to each other.

Although I was able to get another sales job in the same industry the pay wasn't as great and I had to cover several Midwestern states, in the dead of winter, with below zero temperatures, driving through desolate towns to see client's whose offices, sometimes sat in the middle of nowhere.

After eight months of snow, below zero days and bleak weather for months at a time, I had had enough and told Chris I wanted to move back to Florida. He decided to put his home on the market which was expensive to maintain and turn his remaining client's over to a former employee and move back South with me.

Within three months we moved down to the Florida Keys. It was not my ideal place to live for someone used to working in a professional environment but because he found a job first in the marine industry which I had helped him get by creating a resume for him and sending out his cover letters, I didn't complain.

I just wanted out of the cold. Plus, the relationship had been under considerable strain and I didn't want to be stranded in the Midwest should things not have worked out.

Just over a year after moving back to Florida the relationship had run its course. I suspected him of cheating and in my opinion, lying to cover his tracks. Also his total disregard for the financial hardships I was now suffering due to low paying jobs I had to take while living in paradise was another huge factor. Once I no longer had the great income and was barely making above minimum wage, I believe, I had lost my value in his eyes.

Even when I could barely pay my share of the rent and he could afford to pay all of it because of his new job and promotion he refused to help me and demanded that I get two more jobs, if necessary, to make ends meet which I refused to do since I was already working 40 hours a week at my hourly day job.

When the company he worked for was looking for an Office Manager, a job I clearly qualified for and was paying a great salary, he refused to recommend me. He didn't want us working together even though it would have lifted much of my financial burdens and we probably wouldn't have fought as much over money.

He threatened to kick me out on several occasions when we fought over everything from the way he disrespected me to finances even though I was on the lease and furnishing the apartment we lived in with my furniture. And, when I confronted him about my suspicions of his cheating he told me I was crazy, paranoid and insecure.

I gave myself a month to get out of there and out of the Florida Keys. It cost a small fortune to get my furniture and belongings out of such a remote area on my low income salary but since he was staying in our apartment I was not entitled to a reimbursement of my $1600 security deposit so I used that last month there to gather the money I needed to make my move.

I put my furniture in storage temporarily and went to stay with my parents. I could finally be at peace even though I had doubts about the future and what I was going to do next. I still had my barely above minimum wage job that allowed me to work from home anywhere in the country so I at least had a steady income coming in.

It takes courage to leave a bad situation. Your doubts and fears may try and talk you out of leaving even though you know that staying is only going to make things worse. My advice is never stay in a toxic relationship just to say you have someone or because you're afraid of being alone or feeling fearful that you won't find anyone else.

Starting over, in your forties, broke and broken like I was, can be overwhelming, especially if many of your closest friends have turned their back on you. I had very little local support, except one friend who came down from Ft. Lauderdale, God bless her, to help me pack and to offer moral support.

Anyone who learned about my breakup, but didn't really know the details, would always tell me how sorry they were with a tinge of pity in their voices. I found this strange since I wasn't sorry about the breakup. I was relieved to be out of what had become an unbearable situation and grieving over the choices I had made that brought me to this point, at this stage of my life.

I was grieving for myself and for the pain that I had been caused. I was grieving for all the women who were suffering a similar fate and the emotional turmoil we have all endured at the hands of selfish men who only care about their needs and their desires and make us out to be crazy and unstable.

If you happen to be in a similar situation, hopefully, you will feel inspired to get out of that toxic relationship and move forward with your own life, finally finding some peace and happiness. Once I let go and let God guide me I was literally able to get back on my feet within months even though I encountered many roadblocks along the way.

Not only do I feel more at peace but it shows on my face as well. Instead of focusing on a broken relationship I have been able to focus on myself; my health, well-being, and doing whatever I can to look and feel the best that I can at this stage of my life. I definitely feel younger and my body is more fit as I turn all that negative energy that surrounded me in my past into a positive experience.

There were lots of tears and days when I thought I wasn't going to make it after losing so much emotionally and financially and other days where I was full of anger and bitterness at how I was treated.

I couldn't believe that someone that professed to love me could turn suddenly and become so cold, ruthless and uncaring and how I allowed myself to be seduced so easily into that relationship.

I learned how to forgive and move on with my life because if I allowed myself to remain in a negative state of mind, living in a world of darkness, I wouldn't have been able to see the light that would guide me to bigger and better things.

And, because my journey has taught me forgiveness and I have had time to heal and learn from my past, when the time is right, I will be able to love again fully without bringing any of that old baggage with me. And you can do the same.

Its amazing what you can accomplish in your life once you let go of the hurt and pain others have caused you. When you remain in that unhealthy state you're stuck in a sort of paralysis of indecision as you sit and do nothing until several more months or even years have passed.

There is a process that needs to be followed in order to heal and learn to love again. If you ended one relationship and think you are ready to jump into another one you haven't allowed yourself time to figure out what you want next for your life and will repeat the same cycle of wasted years in a relationship that isn't right for you.

We are not in our twenties any longer so we certainly don't want to waste any more precious time with the wrong person. Toxic relationships usually consume us and we may even have lost our own identities as we attempted to morph ourselves into the person we thought our significant other wanted us to be. We spent so much time trying to please him that we lost sight of ourselves.

Due to the nature of those relationships we may even have lost our creative drive to do the things that brought us personal happiness and fulfillment. I loved to sing and write and the last year of my relationship was barely spent doing either of those things. I was too consumed with playing private detective.

I hated the person I had become because that was so beneath me and the secure, self confident woman that I had always believed myself to be. I spent months trying to crack a phone code Chris had suddenly put on his phone that hadn't been there for the 2 1/2 years we had been together and I believe, a sure sign that he was hiding something. I was exhausting myself mentally trying to figure out whom he was seeing behind my back.

This was all very tiring and it started to take a toll on me physically and emotionally. I started losing weight and having stomach problems. I couldn't sleep and kept waking up in the middle of the night and had lost my joy for life.

I remember taking long walks and would literally think of hurling myself off the bridge so I could end the pain and sadness I was experiencing with the downturn my life had taken. But my faith in God kept me going until I was able to get the courage to finally leave even though I had no concrete plans and wasn't sure about my future.

Some of you may have made the decision that enough is enough and you have no interest in ever getting married again or being in a serious relationship. The 2010 U.S. Census Bureau stated that married couples make up less than half of the American households and in all, 31 million Americans live alone, mostly by choice.

These are not people who are embittered and so have chosen the single life for good, but men and women who are completely satisfied with their single lives and are not interested in being in another relationship.

But, for those of us who enjoy having someone in our lives and would like an opportunity to try again and find that special someone that we can spend our lives with, there is no better time than the present.

Forty is the new twenty and if we ignore the grim media statistics there is no reason, when the time is right, that we can't find the person who will be the love of our lives.

If you are suffering from a break-up or a single woman over 40 struggling and trying to figure out where you belong, and if you will ever meet anyone else, there are steps you can take in this book to reclaim your self confidence and learn to feel empowered again.

These qualities are already inside of you and just need to be brought forward. Your ex husband or boyfriend was attracted to you because of these qualities and someone else will be too. You will be able to move on and achieve your dreams and yes, even find a new partner when you're ready.

For now, embrace the journey. Even if it's a difficult one. I promise you it will get better.

Part 1

Courage & Faith

Chapter One
Suddenly Single, Now What?

Being single and in your forties can pose new challenges especially if you spent the last fifteen years or so raising a family and putting their needs first. Whether happily single or not, you are now in a position to create a life that will bring you the greatest fulfillment.

One of my favorite authors, also in her mid-forties, Elizabeth Wurtzel, who wrote Bitch: In Praise Of Difficult Women and Prozac Nation, wrote an article for *New York Magazine* on January 14, 2013, describing what being single felt like for her and with whom I could identify.

"At 44 my life was not so different from the way it was at 24. Stubbornly and proudly, emphatically and pathetically, I had refused to grow up." She went on to say, "that by never marrying, I ended up never divorcing, but I also failed to accumulate that brocade of civility and padlock of security – kids you do or don't want, Tiffany silverware you never use – that makes life complete. Convention serves a purpose. It gives life meaning, and without it, one is in a constant existential crisis."

Certainly, being single can make us feel like we are in constant crisis and create feelings of vulnerability. Being married and in a healthy relationship creates a unity and a bond that both can draw strength from during difficult times.

We long for that person whom we can spend our lives with who will love us unconditionally and be involved in the decision making process. Someone we can bounce ideas off of and who can be the voice of reason when we are unsure about some aspect of our life. But, in order to find that person, we have to get over the wrong one and prepare ourselves for the right one.

If you were in an unhealthy relationship that you knew you needed to get out of for your own sanity and well-being it can create a paralyzing fear as you are suddenly over-whelmed with so many decisions that need to be made.

When I decided it was time to leave my relationship after 2 1/2 years, instead of making plans to get out, I kept hoping things would get better while at the same time feeling anger and resentment toward Chris and frustrated that he continued to lie and shut me out.

I kept prolonging the inevitable because I had become used to living in my dysfunctional environment even though I knew it was not healthy and no longer working for me.

But, at some point, we all get to our "I've had it" moment where we just can't take it anymore. In July, 2013, I realized that nothing was going to mend this broken relationship and I finally started making plans to leave. I gave myself one month to get out.

Fortunately, I had a job that would allow me to work remotely from anywhere in the U.S. I knew I didn't want to stay in the Florida Keys and with much thought and soul searching decided to leave Florida altogether, for a while, as most of my friends had basically turned their backs on me, all except two.

I made the decision to move in temporarily with my parents. In this way, I could give myself time to think clearly and figure out where I wanted to settle next for the interim.

I wasn't making a rash decision to move somewhere I may not have loved living and I no longer made excuses about not leaving because I couldn't figure out where I was going.

Once I set a move date with a moving company there were days that I was crippled with fears and doubts, wondering if I was making the right decision, and not trusting myself to make any decisions.

But, I kept pushing forward even when I didn't feel like it. I kept showing up at work, even when I had to take bathroom breaks so I could cry from being overwhelmed by all that needed to be done to extricate myself from my relationship.

I didn't allow myself to wallow in self pity and I wouldn't allow myself to fall into despair and depression. I had to keep moving forward even though it was painful at times when all I wanted to do was close myself off in a dark room and not see the bright light of day.

I lived in a tropical paradise but I was never able to fully enjoy it. And there were days that I wished the sun didn't shine so brightly, that it would thunderstorm or that black clouds would roll in to match my mood at the time.

To keep my sanity I took daily walks after work. Being around nature and the ocean helped keep me calm and by the time I had made plans to leave I didn't think of hurling myself off a bridge any longer because I now had a plan.

There will be days where you feel crippled with fear and days where you just want to close yourself off from the world but the quicker you can get out of your situation the better you will start to feel. Prolonging an unhealthy living situation is never a good option.

To help you get moving here are a few suggestions that helped me.

Make a plan and stick with it no matter what. Figure out what you can afford on your own and immediately start looking for places to live. If you need to move in temporarily with family or friends then use that as an option.

Before I left Florida altogether I took a day trip up too Orlando and across the state to Tampa and St. Petersburg, all in one day looking at possible places to call home.

Everything was out of my price range at the time and I couldn't afford to pay movers to get my furniture out of the Keys plus pay for a deposit on an apartment so moving in with my parents was the next best thing and a temporary solution. Plus, during times like these you really need to be around supportive people.

If you can't get family and friends to help you move call around until you can find an affordable moving company that fits your budget and negotiate for the best rates. Then set a move date and stick with it.

Don't allow doubt to creep in and make you believe you are making the wrong decision. The fear you may feel will pass but staying in an unbearable situation will never get better.

Enlist a few close friends or your church group to come over and help you pack. You won't feel so overwhelmed if you have help and they can offer you the emotional support you may be lacking.

If necessary, find a therapist to talk with who specializes in relationships or read a good personal development book that will offer you encouragement and keep you focused on moving forward.

When I lived in the Florida Keys my options were extremely limited for just about everything from shopping to finding a decent doctor or therapist. I know I needed someone to talk to about my situation and did not want to overwhelm my parents with my relationship issues.

So I did the next best thing, I bought and downloaded books by Joyce Meyers and Joel Osteen. I highlighted important passages that seemed to speak directly to me and what I was going through.

When the feelings of fear and doubt would creep in I would re-read those highlighted passages and I also prayed, which I did every night anyway, but prayed specifically for guidance and strength to get through this.

This is why it is vitally important to choose carefully when entering a relationship and to weigh your options, pay attention to warning signs, and determine if his lifestyle will be the best fit for yours.

When we are in our forties we don't want to spend the next ten to twenty years trying to get it right when it comes to men and relationships. Chris humiliated me in so many ways, publicly and privately, that I started praying to God asking him simply, "why?"

One passage in Joel Osteen's book, *Become A Better You*, gave me the answer. The passage stated, "sometimes when you go through persecution and rejection, its not always because somebody has it in for you. Sometimes that's God's way of directing you into his perfect will. He's trying to get you to stretch to the next level and he knows you're not going to go without a push."

We can get quite comfortable in our dysfunctional comfort zones while leading lives of quiet desperation. We can talk ourselves out of leaving environments that are unhealthy and continue to stay right where we are, miserable and unhappy.

The unknown is frightening but that is where faith and God's word from the bible can come in handy. In Ecclesiastes 11:4 it states, "if you wait for perfect conditions, you will never get anything done." There will never be a perfect time when it comes to the inevitable. It's uncomfortable, it's annoying, it's frustrating, stressful and life-changing.

We have to believe God has a much better plan for our lives. As his daughters he doesn't want to see us suffer a moment longer in a situation that he knows we need to move on from.

Once you actually set the wheels in motion, take one moment and one day at a time. The worst thing you can do is focus on the unknown and the "what if's". Just because you're suddenly single doesn't mean your life is over or that you will never find anybody else.

Take this time to concentrate on making a new life for yourself and getting settled in your new surroundings. When you find yourself getting depressed, feeling down or feeling sorry for yourself or replaying the same old movie in your head, change the channel and focus on something else.

Moving in with my parents, temporarily, after having been married and running my own household was a difficult adjustment to make. I could have focused on the negatives but I chose to appreciate the fact that I was now surrounded by people who genuinely loved me and had my best interest at heart. I also became very close to my four year old niece whom I adored.

She kept me entertained and busy as we played with her dolls, legos, and whatever else her little mind could think of throughout the course of the day. Sometimes she would have a sleep over at my parents house and would sleep curled up next to me.

She always told me how much she loved her "Auntie Michelle" and asked lots of inquisitive questions for a four year old about my previous life in Florida. It was hard to be sad and depressed around this beautiful little girl and I think she helped save my life in a sense. As difficult as this may be, find it within yourself to be happy and the reason why will come.

By holding it together, walking in faith, being surrounded by loving people and not focusing on all the negatives that took place, I was able to quickly move forward. And, if I can do it, so can you.

God will be there with you every step of the way. If you pray and don't get an answer right away, don't give up on God. He will answer when the time is right. And, when you don't see his footprints in the sand, know that is when he is carrying you.

Step #1:

Reclaiming Yourself

As you make your way out into the world as a single woman visualize where you want to live and what you see yourself doing within the next year. Do you want to start your own business? Go back to school? Become a consultant? What are you passionate about? Make a list and once you get settled in your new surroundings start taking steps to make those dreams come true. Keep the focus on your personal desires and you will have less time to think about the broken relationship you left behind.

Chapter Two
Life Isn't Over After 40

Now that you're single everyone from parents, siblings and friends will want to put their two cents in and predict your future chances of finding someone when you're over forty.

The internet has forecast which U.S. cities have the best chances of meeting single men over forty. And online dating services compete for our attention by guaranteeing that their site has the most marriages out of any other online dating site.

A cover story written by *Newsweek* back in 1986 called "The Marriage Crunch" and still being circulated on the internet today, claimed that a forty year old college educated woman was more likely to die in a terrorist attack than meet a man and get married at her age.

Of course, back in 1986 we were still in high school and probably didn't give this much thought as we still had our entire lives ahead of us. But the damage was done and little did we know, this article would come to define, shape and stereotype women over 40 today.

And, create this stigma that there is a shortage of men, compared to available and single women and that all the good ones are already married. So even with the invention of online dating we are supposedly, out of luck because the men that are available are either not looking for a serious relationship or are not relationship material.

Sometimes, even the place where we feel most safe as a single woman can make us feel uncomfortable and insecure on occasion. A recent message presented one particular Sunday at church was about focusing on relationships and strengthening one's marriage. The pastor talked about how our husband should be our best friend, someone who has our back and is also a provider and shields his household.

I don't think he took into consideration those of us who were single and how uncomfortable this might have felt for us. I was surrounded by couples as the pastor delved deeper into the message and I felt even more alone.

The scriptures supported his sermon as God believes relationships are important to his people which should give us single women hope.

"Two people are better off than one for they can help each other succeed." Ecclesiastes 4:9

"If one person falls, the other can reach out and help. But someone who falls alone is in real trouble." Ecclesiastes 4:10

"A person standing alone can be attacked and defeated, but two can stand back to back and conquer." Ecclesiastes 4:12

Even the bible makes it clear that there are strength in numbers and we could benefit from a partnership. I could have gotten discouraged and fallen back into despair and doubt wondering if I would find the right partner but I know how much God loves us and will grant us the desires of our heart.

If our goal is to have a partner in our life, one that loves, respects and treats us well, then there is no reason why he wouldn't want to answer that prayer. We may not have met him yet but with faith we know that he is out there and we will meet him one day.

If God delivered Eve to Adam, then he can surely bring us the man of our dreams. We have to believe, be patient and trust in him. This is not the time to get impatient and go running into another disastrous relationship.

No matter how much we may be hurting or hate being alone this time should be spent on taking care of ourselves. For some this may mean re-inventing yourself; joining a gym, getting a makeover, working on your personal development, starting a business or a new career. Take up the challenge and let this be an exciting time for you to decide what you want out of life and what you want to do for the rest of your life.

Don't get caught up in all the negative reports written online about how awful it is for single women over 40. Those writers are entitled to their opinion but that doesn't mean it will apply to you and your life.

Someone recently posted on their blog that women over forty start to lose their intelligence. Hmmm, maybe the guy that wrote that article, is himself, unintelligent and needed to somehow validate his own self worth by making us look stupid. Perhaps he personally dated a woman over 40 who came across as unintelligent and therefore, assumed we are all dumb.

Another blog site claims that women over forty won't be taken seriously by a younger man and that if he does show interest it's only because he wants to sleep with you and not interested in a long term relationship.

The article went on to say that you might as well not bother looking at men in their early forties either because they all want women in their twenties so best to look for men in their fifties and beyond. And, even if you happen to be a hot forty something that won't matter to men because age trumps hotness.

Do not take this type of advice seriously. I have never experienced that and don't know where that woman got her information from except maybe her own experience which she was projecting onto another forty something who contacted her for advice. Every individual's path is different and you may have completely different challenges as a single woman over 40.

You may start noticing friends who are married or still in relationships suddenly start pulling away from you now that you are newly single. When my relationship ended and I needed a shoulder to cry on, my closest friend of over 20 years, even turned her back on me. I was sad and depressed by this because we had been like sisters.

If you happen to be attractive and have friends who are insecure with themselves or their relationship, be prepared if they stop making time for you. I remember Denise telling me, after having not seen me for almost ten years, that I still looked like I did in my twenties and that she hated me for not aging one bit. I hoped she was joking.

Then, one weekend, over the holidays, when I had been invited to stay in her home with her husband and daughter, who treated me like her little sister, her husband fondly made a comment that I looked like one of the Bratz Dolls. By the following day I could tell Denise was feeling uncomfortable with me being there and I decided to leave. I didn't want to upset her or make her feel uncomfortable.

But I think we were both feeling insecure for different reasons. I envied her for having a husband and child and the love that they shared as a family making her feel safe and secure while I felt vulnerable and alone.

And I think she envied me because of the freedom I had to come and go as I pleased. Plus, I didn't have children and the responsibilities that went with raising a child that she hadn't been prepared for in her early forties.

We can feel like the whole world has turned their backs on us during this time and feel even more alone. You may even feel the urge to jump back out there and find someone new as quickly as you can.

But do yourself a favor. Don't settle for less than you deserve. Give yourself time to heal from a broken heart or just from an emotionally draining relationship, even if your heart wasn't broken.

You may still be harboring anger and bitterness and reliving what went wrong in a previous relationship which is normal. But only time can heal those wounds and you won't be doing yourself or your new love any good if you bring all those past hurts into a new relationship.

How much time will you need? You will know when the time is right because your heart won't feel heavy any more. You will feel more at peace and carefree and when the sun shines brightly you will actually welcome it instead of trying to shut it out behind dark curtains.

You will have taken some time to figure out what went wrong in your old relationship and be able to take ownership of your part. Even if he was the one running around cheating, what could you have done to handle things differently?

I wasted precious energy trying to catch Chris at his own game and when I couldn't outright catch him in the act I became frustrated and angry because I felt he was getting over on me and I wasn't going to let that happen.

We lived in such a small town that I felt everyone knew what he was doing behind my back because when we would go out to dinner or meet up with some of his co-workers they would give me pitiful or strange looks which I picked up on and couldn't do anything about.

Chris constantly blamed his ex-wife for the demise of their relationship and never once took ownership for his part. He accused her of being a terrible mother who was constantly cheating on him, when they were married and talked about how unattractive she was. He claimed she would leave him to care for their young children while she went out partying several nights a week.

In my opinion, not only did he paint himself as "dad of the year", he constantly put this woman down throughout the 2 1/2 years I was with him and never took any personal responsibility for his young daughter's troubled behavior.

If that wasn't bad enough, within two months of my departure, a mutual friend contacted me from his home town, and told me he had plastered pictures all over his Facebook page of him and his new girlfriend whom he professed to be madly in love with, after only a few short months. She was the spitting image of his ex-wife whom he claimed to despise and found physically repulsive. Go figure!

I had already moved on from that relationship and wasn't experiencing any heartache that he had found someone else so quickly. Nor was I surprised. He was constantly going out of town for the day when we had been together so it was probably someone he had already been seeing while he was still with me. I certainly didn't envy her and what she had gotten herself into.

I had given myself time to heal and had gotten past the anger and hurt I felt toward this man and myself for ignoring all the warning signs that could have saved me from making irrational decisions that cost me my career and my bank account. I had to learn to forgive although it didn't happen overnight.

During the two years that my relationship was slowly unraveling, I had three of my friends meet the man of their dreams and get married. It was hard to look at their smiling faces on Facebook and see all the beautiful pictures of their wedding day.

At least two of them had experienced the same struggles as I had in trying to find a decent guy and we all met our partners around the same time. But while my relationship was falling apart, for a brief moment, I envied them for their choices, while regretting my own.

But I wasn't going to allow myself to believe that there was a man shortage and that it would be almost impossible to find any good, single men because they were all taken and if they weren't, that something must be wrong with them.

And who said we had to find someone in our specific age group? Being in our forties is actually an advantage because we can date up in age or date someone younger. It all depends on you and the type of person you can see yourself spending your life with. In my previous relationships, both men were younger. There goes that theory that age trumps hotness!

I possess a young spirit and dress a lot younger than my age but not in an inappropriate and unflattering way. Standing next to a twenty something no one would know the difference. And that's what makes many of us not look like your typical woman in her forties.

We take better care of ourselves, eat healthy, have a passion for life and are not experiencing the midlife crises that some men and women experience who are married.

Married couples have greater responsibilities especially if they have children and a household to run and don't always make time for each other which can contribute to one or the other going through a mid-life crises. As single women we have the freedom to experience and enjoy life to the fullest without the burdens that a household and children can bring.

It took me a long time to realize that even in my current single state that I no longer have to feel insecure or worry about how others perceive me, especially old friends, who haven't seen me in a while and are shocked when they find out I am not married. Give me a break, I've only been single for a few months. And, marriage is no guarantee of happily ever after either.

Someone could go through the motions of planning the most spectacular wedding, inviting hundreds of guests, buying the most breathtaking wedding gown, going on the most romantic of honeymoons and then end up separated and divorced a year later. So don't pity us or feel like you're superior because you are married because in this day and age nothing is guaranteed.

I no longer allow my single status to define who I am as a person because I know this status can change at any time. This time spent alone now is a small price to pay considering a life time spent with the man of my dreams in the coming future.

Step 2:

What Makes You Unique & Different

How would you describe yourself right now? What strengths and qualities do you possess that make you unique and different from everyone else? How can these qualities serve you now as a single woman and help propel you forward as you take the steps needed to start a new life?

Chapter Three
Identity Crises

One thing that we tend to do as women when we are in a relationship is completely alter our lives to fit the person we are with. As women, we are more willing to change our lifestyle to fit theirs even if we are not married to them. The more unhealthy the relationship becomes the harder we try to please and be what we think they want us to be.

By the time the relationship is over we may have lost sight of who we are and what was important to us before we got involved with the person we were with. Family and friends may have made comments like, "you've changed" or "you just don't seem like your old self", or "I don't like the person you've become".

Someone may ask you what you intend to do now that the relationship has ended and you may draw a blank. It's been so long since you did anything for you that mattered.

We can easily lose our own identity in a relationship and this isn't healthy. No matter whom you may end up meeting in the future it's so important to have things going on in your life that bring you personal happiness. Even if we end up marrying the man of our dreams, and have much in common, we should still give each other some space to pursue our hobbies.

I enjoy horseback riding. I don't know many men that do unless they are Polo players or own their own horses. I love riding my motorcycle on a beautiful spring or summer day.

Not every guy knows how to ride a motorcycle. I also enjoy shopping and working out. I wouldn't think of dragging a guy to the mall while I go shopping if it's something he doesn't enjoy doing.

One thing I managed not to do was to lose my identity completely with my ex boyfriend when we were together. I joined an all girls singing group which was quite popular and well known in the Florida Keys. I spent a lot of time rehearsing and learning new dance routines for public performances.

This was during the time when I felt my relationship was in greater turmoil and my mind would often wander thinking if he was somewhere cheating on me while I was down in Key West rehearsing. But, I kept doing what I loved anyway.

But, there were other times where I felt completely drained mentally and had lost my creative drive to write which I had enjoyed so much. I went almost an entire year without writing anything meaningful.

I would start projects and abandon them just as quickly when things were going sour in my relationship. I spent way to much time trying to analyze what went wrong. And, ended up blocking my own ability to be the creative force that I knew was still inside of me.

We may have had some form of an identity crises during our unhealthy relationships and need to reclaim that part of our personalities that make us unique and special and probably what drew that person to us to begin with.

Your personality shapes your behavior and is the driving force behind what motivates you to do things you enjoy doing. It's what makes you different and appealing to the opposite sex and reinforces the part of you that is exciting, bold, sexy and attractive.

It's important to maintain your hobbies and take the time to learn new skills or brush up on old ones. And never apologize for doing something you love that brings you personal satisfaction. We should never compromise who we are in these areas of our lives.

You want to be in a position to stand up for yourself in every situation and not be afraid to shine and utilize your God given talents. The guy who really loves you will support you and encourage you in your efforts.

I've always enjoyed singing and was even pursuing it as a profession at one time. I was chosen to sing with the Palm Beach Opera and selected to play the role of Carmen in the Palm Beach Opera Studio in Concert series, providing a peek into the Palm Beach Opera's 41st season opener.

I was also a lead singer with a contemporary christian rock band called The Faithful, started by Mark, my ex boyfriend of thirteen years and myself, where I wrote and co-produced many of the band's songs, on our first CD called, *Bearing Good Fruit*.

When I started dating Chris I assumed he would support me in my musical endeavors by being encouraging and supportive but he seemed uncomfortable with this area of my life that meant so much to me.

Had I been with the right partner, at the time, he would have been proud of my accomplishments and talents as a singer and performer. As much as he liked to say I was an insecure person because I suspected him of cheating, an insecure person would not have been on stage dancing and singing with confidence, sometimes in front of thousands of people and for special appearances such as CNN Live for the New Year's Eve shoe drop.

If anything he was insecure in the world that I inhabited as a performer and although he would say, "great job" there wasn't much conviction behind his words and they didn't ring true. But I was proud of myself for not giving up on the one thing that kept me going and gave me a reason to get out of bed every morning during that time.

By having hobbies and interests, when you meet someone new you will sound much more interesting and have much more to talk about. Men find this more desirable than a woman who comes across as needy or worse, boring because she doesn't appear to have a life outside of her job.

Set your standards high even if you're great at doing a lot of different things. Some men may be intimidated by all of your abilities but never play down your talents. I dated a guy once who told me that he didn't like dating a woman who was smarter than himself. I was way too receptive and intelligent and he didn't like this. Apparently, he liked his women to look good but preferred them to be dumb and stupid.

Not every guy you meet will appreciate hearing about all of your talents and abilities especially if they haven't accomplished as much and may feel intimidated. So, allow him to do the talking first and find out about his interests and accomplishments before revealing your own.

Going forward I have decided to gradually reveal my talents and abilities and in this way it will come as more of a wonderful surprise and he won't be made to feel insignificant if he hasn't accomplished as much in his personal life.

Get clear on exactly what you want for your life. Stick with your plan and do a little each day that will have you reaching your goals before you know it. You will become a stronger person and won't be completely consumed by your other half the next time around.

Step 3:

How Much Time Are You Willing To Invest In Yourself?

If you've spent the last several years living under someone else's shadow now is the time to re-evaluate your dreams and goals. Ask yourself the following questions:

What am I good at? What have I always wanted to do? What skills or classes do I need to take to fulfill my dreams? How much time and money am I willing to invest in obtaining a better life for myself?

Chapter Four
Battling Loneliness

Feeling lonely is a state of mind and being alone isn't the same thing as feeling lonely. Once you have lived at home for a while, like I did, you truly appreciate your own space when you get settled into your new surroundings.

After living with my parents for several months I couldn't wait to move into my own place. I appreciated all their support helping me get back on my feet. God bless them, but they were also helping my step-sister who lived there for a while, who was also in her forties, and her dysfunctional twenty year old son. And, a twenty-three year old family friend who had lost her mother and was not coping well.

I was looking forward to some peace and quiet and just being able to think and process everything I had recently gone through myself. But, because our family friend had lost her mother, I became like a sister to her and was able to take the focus off myself and offer her some comfort during that time.

I was ready to move forward with my life and moved into my new place with minimum furniture until I could afford to have my stuff brought up from Florida. I had moved almost two hours away from my family, in a new city that I was unfamiliar with and no friends. But, I quickly found a church to join which helped, and got me out of my apartment and around other people.

But, weekends, at first, were sometimes hard, being alone with no friends in town yet, to fill my evenings. I resisted the urge to rush back to my parents every weekend to fill that gap. I knew this was something I needed to go through on my own. I ended up spending both Christmas Eve and Christmas Day completely alone as I had to work both days.

I had never spent the holidays alone before and it was somewhat depressing. I dressed up and went to church on Christmas Eve. I sat surrounded by families in my aloneness and sang beautiful Christmas carols as tears welled up in my eyes. I was grateful that it was dimly lit as the service was held by candlelight.

Christmas day was spent working eight hours from home but at least I was able to stay in my pajamas all day while I made reservations for families and couples planning their vacations. I was grateful for my best friend who called me from Florida and we spent a few hours talking on the phone.

I thought back to last christmas which had been as bad as it could get. I had flown to the Midwest with Chris to visit his children. We stayed at his parent's house and had to sleep on a makeshift bed in the living room with no privacy.

We fought continually over money. He had brought his dog and wanted me to pay the $150 to get the dog back home on the plane. I told him I needed the money to find a dress for my CNN New Year's Eve performance and couldn't pay for both. His mother, tired of our bickering, gave me a gift card to get my dress and I ended up paying for the dog's flight home.

We went to his brother's house on Christmas Eve. It was a sad occasion as his brother and his wife were getting a divorce. He had been cheating on her with her best friend and next door neighbor. They ended up fighting and we ended up going home. I couldn't help but think this was probably the last time I would see his family as our relationship wasn't much better.

So even though this past Christmas had been spent in solitude at least I wasn't stressed out and fighting with someone who really didn't want to be with me and had been feeling resentful that he had to pay for my ticket to go visit his family in the first place.

There will be times when you may actually feel lonely but I promise they will be fleeting if you keep busy, focus on your goals and make an effort to get out there and meet other people either through a local Meet up group, church or gym.

There will be other times when you feel the urge to jump back out there in the dating world just so you won't feel so lonely. I resisted this urge until I knew I was ready. Instead of allowing my emotions to take the lead, I decided to think logically and not put myself out there just because I had bouts of loneliness.

During those times we may feel sorry for ourselves and get depressed. The hardest part for me had been sleeping alone and it took me a long time to feel comfortable again, alone, in my own bed. I thought about getting a small dog but decided against it for the time being.

Some of you may even welcome the solitude. And feeling lonely may not even be an issue. I work from home five days a week, eight hours a day, so at the end of my work day I can't wait to get out of the house and be around other people.

I had also decided to take a part-time job as a hostess at a local Italian restaurant, for a little while anyway, so I could meet more of the locals. It also gave me a reason to dress up and I didn't have to worry about being alone on a Friday or Saturday night until I started making new friends.

When you start feeling lonely and thoughts enter your head making you question the decision you made to leave an unhappy relationship or you feel the urge to rush out and take that gorgeous, unavailable guy, up on his offer to get together, I urge you not to lose your head and make a rash decision that will leave you even more emotionally vulnerable.

Take all that energy and those negative thoughts and do something constructive that will put you in a different frame of mind. Go for a nice long walk, put in a favorite movie, put on some music and dance around your apartment or go and work up a good sweat at the gym. Or call up a girlfriend and get together and go shopping, talking about anything other than men and relationships.

Once you get moving, dancing, singing, working up a sweat, laughing with a girlfriend or spending time with your family you won't feel sad and lonely for long and those negative thoughts will start to fade away.

I don't have any children so moving within driving distance of my family allowed me the opportunity to spend quality time with my four year old niece and nephew whom I adore and who loves me, equally, in return.

I didn't want to make this a long drawn out chapter because I don't want you dwelling on feeling lonely. Just know that we all go through those stages and it's normal. Even couples in relationships tend to feel lonely if their partner is constantly neglecting them so rest assured being lonely isn't just something that single people experience.

Keep working on developing your skills, pursue your dreams and hobbies and make new friends with other singles and you won't have time to feel lonely for long. And, as the days and months pass quickly by, the hurt and pain you have been experiencing will become a distant memory.

Step 4:

What Makes You Happy Personally?

Not, what makes your kids happy or friends happy but you personally? Make a list and put it somewhere where you can find it quickly should you have those days where you feel alone and need something constructive to do that will distract you from sad or destructive thoughts.

Chapter Five

Letting Go Of Bitterness And Anger

Letting go of bitterness and anger can be extremely difficult especially if you were betrayed by a cheating partner or spouse. If allowed, these feelings can consume you and eat away at your peace of mind.

When a relationship ends without closure or a spouse tells you, quite suddenly, that he's met someone else and leaving, it can leave you stunned and shocked, stirring up emotions of anger, bitterness and hurt that can stay with you for a long time.

Personally, I think the signs of a troubled relationship reveal themselves early on but are often overlooked or ignored which is a big mistake. When there are problems and couples don't like to deal with them immediately it can cause issues to escalate in a relationship.

But, when it's over you have no choice but to deal with moving on while also dealing with suddenly having to let go. We want that person to pay for hurting us, we want retribution or an absolution that may never come.

We want to see that person suffer, in some way, to help us feel somehow better that they got what they deserved. Hang on to those negative emotions for too long and that anger and bitterness will start to shape you into a person you and others around you may not like.

Nine months into my 2 1/2 year relationship brought about the most incredible challenges that I could ever have imagined that took it's toll on me mentally and emotionally.

Because my partner and I were in a long distance relationship we had decided that I would leave West Palm Beach, FL and move all my furniture and belongings to the Midwest, just as winter was starting, to live with him in his home. Crazy idea, right?

Every other weekend I played step-mum to his preteen daughter whom I adored and his teenage son who was a delight. But, I hadn't been there a month before I noticed his daughter acting strange. She had come to visit me several times, in Florida, with her dad and seemed fine. But now she was more withdrawn and angry.

Her mother informed us that she was cutting herself which explained why she always wore long sleeve sweaters or jackets all the time even in the house. Her arms were covered in cuts; some were healing and others were red and sore.

I remember that weekend in particular, it was our weekend to have her and we took her to the hospital. The ER doctor suggested we get her psychiatric help. I felt helpless since I wasn't her real mother and my comments about how could this happen to such a young girl and suggestions about how to help her were not always welcomed or appreciated by my boyfriend.

I was having a hard time adapting to living in my new environment, in the dead of winter, working a new job that required me to cover several states as a sales consultant, plus figure out how I could be of help to his daughter all while lacking emotional support of my own.

Understandably, my boyfriend had to spend all his free time concentrating on getting his daughter the help she needed but I started to feel neglected and the relationship began to suffer as I was left to deal with my own pain and misery and also upset that his daughter was going through so much pain of her own at such a young age.

He and his ex-wife attended parenting classes for emotionally disturbed children. I attended one of these classes and thought how sad it was that these parents had children they couldn't figure out how to help or handle.

There was the constant bed wetting and the disrespect she showed both her mother and her father, the cutting, and the flirtatious behavior in school were all signs, in my personal opinion, of some form of personal trauma.

I tried to discuss the issue with Chris so we could determine what could have caused this behavior. I also approached the subject with his mother. Although concerned, she didn't really know how to help her granddaughter who shut almost everyone out and brushed aside my theories.

During all of this I also suspected he was once again cheating on me. He would suddenly alter his appearance or lie to me about early morning meetings he had. When I confronted him he would get angry and defensive and threaten to kick me out, in the dead of winter.

But, just as quickly, he would get over his anger and be nice again. I continued to have doubts about his fidelity and would confront his suspicious behavior which happened at least two to three times a month.

He continued to get defensive, curse me out and had even put his hand up once, as if he was going to strike me, and again, threatened to kick me to the curb. I wasn't afraid of him and stood my ground but this was no way to live.

I thought of packing up and moving back to Florida on several occasions but held back because I knew it would be expensive trying to get my furniture and belongings out of there. And it wasn't going to be easy finding another job and a place to live. So, I stayed and paid the price.

On January 1st, 2012, I woke up with what appeared to be a rash developing on one side of my face. Then I got a severe ear ache and started not feeling well. Two days later the rash had developed into open sores on my face and now underneath my eyelid so that it hurt terribly to even blink.

I could barely see out of my right eye and decided to get to an eye doctor immediately. I scheduled a dermatology appointment for the following day to figure out what this strange rash was covering half of my face.

I never made it to that dermatology appointment. The eye doctor took one look at me and pronounced that I had the shingles on my face and in my right eye. Had I waited to come in for treatment even two days later I could possibly have caused permanent nerve damage in that eye and possibly lost my eyesight. I was given a prescription of antibiotics and strong steroid eyedrops.

I was told my rashes would get worse before they got better. Basically they would become open, oozing sores that would eventually dry out and crust up and fall off. I had never heard of the shingles before moving to the Midwest. But, apparently, anyone who has had the chickenpox carries the virus which was brought on, in my case, by severe stress, according to my doctor.

The move across country with no family or friends for moral support, trying to adjust to a new environment, new job, and deal with Chris's daughter's emotional problems, plus the stress of his mood swings and suspected infidelity had taken a severe toll on my own health.

For over a month I couldn't leave the house except for weekly doctor appointments. I had to stay in bed all day in complete darkness because the light hurt my eyes. The pain was terrible.

My face looked like a monster with open sores that were draining fluid. I couldn't go to work and had to cancel all of my appointments including an important visit that was scheduled with my new bosses who were in town.

I would lay in bed feeling helpless and depressed and wondering why I made such a terrible decision to move to this desolate area in the first place. I cried all the time.

Surprisingly, both my boyfriend and his daughter were sympathetic and compassionate. How he laid next to me every night with my open sores draining, I will never know, but it still brought me little comfort or relief.

Once my face started to heal and the sores dried up and turned into scabs, I was left with scarring that took almost six months to clear up. I had to wear a scarf for the first two months and heavy makeup to try and conceal some of the scarring plus large oversize sunglasses because my eyes were still so sensitive to the dreary daylight.

To this day you can still see faint scars on my forehead as a reminder of that fateful time in my life. It will forever be a reminder to never make such a bad decision again when it came to giving up so much of myself for someone that never kept any of his promises even when he presented me with a promise ring.

The house I was living in with him and helping to pay for had very high bills and was financially draining to both of us. I had had enough and told him I wanted to move back to Florida. I was crying hysterically and depressed all the time. I was tired of the snow, the weeks and months of gray skies and the lack of friends.

I had always been a strong person. I grew up in a military household and travelled the world so I usually adjusted quickly to my surroundings but I never adjusted to living in that part of the Midwest probably because the person I was with didn't always make me feel loved and at home.

I never made any close friends in the eight months that I lived there. Although, nice enough, I found most of the people to be frosty, like their state. Not overly warm and friendly, so it was very hard to make new friends. Literally a month before my departure my neighbor across the street came over and finally introduced herself.

She was an artist and a Christian and took a liking to me. She was genuinely upset when she found out I was moving back to Florida after we had just met but as a going away gift she painted me a beautiful floral portrait and wrote the sweetest note on the bottom and back of the canvas.

We were friends with one couple that we spent some time with but they were going through marital problems and our get togethers with them were far and few between. Sadly, their marriage came to an end when the husband, in a drunken state, tried to kill the entire family.

It was front page news at the time. His wife and four children were left in a precarious situation. I had liked them both and was even more saddened at how yet another relationship had come to a bad end.

I remember when my relationship finally ended and I called up Chris's mother to tell her what had happened and how I suspected he had been cheating on me she just said, "sorry for your loss," as if she were talking to a stranger. Now that I was no longer dating her son she suddenly turned cold and indifferent.

So when I finally moved back to Florida that should have been the end of my relationship but my boyfriend decided to short sale the house and move back with me. His children wanted to stay with their mother, and not leave their friends, and so would visit us during holidays and summer break.

I thought this transition would take away a lot of the stress I had felt living in the Midwest and that our relationship would improve since he was now making a sacrifice for me; leaving his home and children behind.

Had they wanted to come with us they would have been welcomed but neither wanted to move South. I learned that when you're with the wrong person, it doesn't matter where you live, nothing will improve a doomed relationship and I started to feel a sense of hopelessness.

I ended up drifting from one low paying hourly job after another as there were no professional jobs to be found in paradise. I was offered a job in Miami working for a wonderful husband and wife team from South America as their Director of Sales & Marketing for their start up health magazine. But, the two hour commute, each way, proved too costly. I had to give up the job I enjoyed because the tolls and gas was eating away at my salary.

During the twelve hours a day, five days a week I had spent working and commuting to Miami for my job, I once again, suspected Chris was cheating on me. It started with subtle things such as him deleting my wall paper photo from his phone and putting up a picture of his new vehicle. Then he put a code on his phone another clear sign that something wasn't right.

Things went from bad to worse as I found more and more condemning evidence that pointed toward him being unfaithful. The times I confronted him were met with anger, denial and harsh words. Nothing I said or did got through to him in any positive way.

By the time I left two months later I was both angry and bitter. Angry that I had invested so much of myself emotionally and financially into that relationship and bitter at the way he ended up treating me in the end.

I remember our very last argument had been over his dog going to the bathroom on my expensive area rug. Since it was going with me I asked him nicely if he would power wash it. And right in front of my best friend and nephew who had come to help me move, he told me quite harshly that I could shove that rug right up my ass because he wasn't going to do anything.

What had happened to the person that I had met in the beginning of our relationship? He had presented himself as this loving, romantic, sensual man who had said all the right things to draw me in and then just a few short years later, turned into this enraged, angry, cold and disrespectful person who could have cared less about me and what he was putting me through.

I had never been spoken to like that in my entire life by any man nor had humiliating things said and done to me which I couldn't even put in this book. So, yes, I can admit it, for a while, I was that bitter and angry woman in her forties. But, not because it was a part of my personality or because I had had a string of bad relationships that caused me to behave that way because I hadn't until I met him.

Chris had completely and utterly destroyed, at the time, what faith I had in relationships and the promise of love that he had so ardently showed me in the beginning of that relationship.

He claimed he had been searching for years for someone like me. Yet, he threw it all away. He had impressed me with a diamond promise ring three months into our relationship to show his devotion to me. So, naturally, I was seduced into believing I had possibly found Prince Charming.

Finding the will to forgive was not easy. But I knew if I didn't find a way to forgive this person I would never acquire peace and happiness and would miss out on any future opportunity to spend my life with someone that I was truly meant to be with. You will never find the right person as long as you stay with the wrong one.

In Colossians 3:13-14, the bible tells us to "bear with each other and forgive whatever grievances you may have against one another. Forgive as the Lord forgave you." As much as we want to see that person suffer, "vengeance is mine saith, The Lord".

Since we make mistakes, screw up and sin just like everyone else how can we ask for forgiveness of our sins yet not forgive others? And, how do we get past this bitterness and anger? By not being self focused. When we are constantly focusing on ourselves and our problems we face continued disappointment.

We obsess over our wronged situation, we encounter loneliness as we shut ourselves off from others and sometimes engage in manipulative behaviors. These are all self-destructive habits.

The best way to get back at someone is to become the best, most successful and attractive person you can be now that you are not with them. This will bring you the most satisfaction and word will eventually get back to him about how well you are doing now that the two of you are no longer together.

I had the pleasure of getting to hear Dr. John C. Maxwell preach at our church, Christ Fellowship, in Palm Beach Gardens, FL.,on many occasions. He suggested that by developing systems they would help us grow.

I determined what areas I needed to work on developing that would help me become a stronger more empowered woman. I needed to stop giving away my power to others. I knew I needed to work on having patience, stop giving up on projects so easily when I became bored or frustrated and stop looking to others for approval.

I also learned to stop worrying about what others thought of me and became better at handling my emotions when situations came up that were stressful. Shortly after moving into my new place someone had started stalking me and I had to deal with the various things this person was doing to cause me grief and aggravation.

I could have allowed these problems to set me back but I continued to persevere with the systems I put in place for myself until I could get to a place where I felt calm even in the midst of chaos and confusion as to who was doing these terrible things to me.

When your life is chaotic and you're not sure what to do or where to turn pray for guidance and direction. Let go of the bitterness and the pain, the hurt and the anger you may feel toward that person. By doing this you can free your mind and stop him from subconsciously having control over you and your thoughts.

Getting rid of bitterness and resentment will open our hearts and de-clutter our minds as we focus on achieving our personal goals and opening ourselves up to receiving all the abundance and goodness God has in store for us.

He can't bless us if we've closed ourselves off to receiving his gifts of love, empathy, compassion, abundance, joy, peace and happiness. So, let go and let God and watch him perform miracles in your life that you could not have imagined or accomplished on your own.

Step 5:

What Steps Can You Take To Forgive The Person Who Hurt You?

What systems can you put into place to help you grow on a daily basis? How can you finally put the past behind you and not dwell on the negative situations that happened when you were in your last relationship? What can you do now to find inner peace and take better care of your needs?

Chapter Six
Leaving Your Past Behind

By refusing to dwell on the past is the only way to help you heal and move forward. Hanging out at your old stomping ground hoping to run into your ex or calling on his friends under false pretenses, driving past his residence or just outright stalking, will not only prolong your hurt and pain but will have you feeling miserable and desperate.

The town I lived in with my ex was a small tourist town where all the locals knew each other. I didn't like living there to begin with so I was happy to leave. I knew if I stayed I would run into him on a regular basis and I didn't need that.

Putting the past behind and pretending it didn't happen is perhaps unrealistic. It takes time to get over emotional pain and there will be times when something triggers an old memory or an unpleasant scene from your past will pop into your head. That's normal. But dwelling on the past and living in the past is not.

Someone sent me a quote that said, "sometimes, the best thing you can do is not think, not wonder, not imagine, not obsess. Just breathe. And have faith that everything will work out for the best."

Keeping a journal and writing down your thoughts and feelings of past experiences and how they made you feel can open your eyes to the reality of your past relationship and remove any blinders for a future relationship.

Imagine, just for a moment, what it would feel like had your relationship been filmed as a reality TV show. How would you have been portrayed? As a victim? Naive? Weak? Wimpy? In denial? Write down an objective view of yourself in that role.

If negative thoughts come to mind then those are the areas you need to work on improving so you can move forward feeling your best, knowing you are no longer that weak minded, naive person but a self confident woman who knows what she wants and will not allow herself to be taken advantage of again in the future.

Only you can decide what steps you need to take first to move forward in your life. You may want to box up old photos, mementos or any other gifts you accumulated during that relationship and put them away until you are able to look at them without getting emotional.

Chris bought me a pre-owned luxury SUV our first christmas together. Many of you may be thinking he couldn't have been all that bad if he was generous with such an extravagant gift! But, his gifts always came at a high price.

I was under so much financial pressure trying to help him pay for his expensive home that I had started to neglect paying my own bills. I had lived in a high-rise condo when he met me and my living expenses were manageable.

But, once I moved into his 3000 square ft. home, in the dead of winter, the heating bills alone were astronomical. I was starting to get harassing phone calls from the finance company wanting payment for my SUV that I was paying for before I met him.

When I mentioned this to him and told him that I was afraid they would come and take my vehicle he told me not to worry about it because they didn't have my physical home address only a mailing address.

I told him there was a tracking device on my vehicle. I was sure of it and asked him to check. He told me I was being paranoid and that we would help me catch up my payments after Christmas.

Well, one day, while out calling on clients, I happened to walk outside in near zero degree weather just as the repo tow truck was hitching up my vehicle to be taken away. I ran over and explained the situation and why the payments hadn't been made.

The woman who accompanied the tow truck felt sorry for me so she actually gave me a ride to a rental car agency as she didn't want to leave me stranded in the freezing weather. My calls to Chris at the time, went unanswered and I noted how he was never around when I needed him most.

I spoke with the finance company while she chauffeured me around town. They were so angry that I had moved out of state without giving them a physical forwarding address that they refused to work with me.

The vehicle had a tracking device but because we lived in such a remote part of the state they couldn't pick up a signal until I came into town. I ended up not getting the vehicle back thanks to Chris so I guess out of guilt he bought me a vehicle and made it clear that he wanted me to pay him back monthly.

The new vehicle was originally in his name since he had paid cash outright for it but was reluctantly switched over into my name once we moved to Florida for insurance purposes.

And when the relationship came to an end I traded in the vehicle for a smaller, more economical car. I didn't need the constant reminders of his "generosity" and couldn't afford the $70 required to fill up the gas tank every time I got on the road.

Should you decide not to part with gifts bestowed to you during a previous relationship make sure those gifts are not constant reminders of what went wrong in the relationship and don't trigger unpleasant thoughts of the past.

And, if you do decide to box up or let go of those gifts know that it's a better alternative than having a constant reminder of what they represented. Believe me once you let go of those material possessions you will feel free to move on knowing the best is yet to come.

Step 6:

What Would Your Reality TV Show Look Like?

You are the star of your own reality TV show. How would your character appear to the public? How would your relationship with your partner be portrayed? How would your final episode of the season end? Be honest in your assessment of yourself as you jot down your thoughts as if you were watching reruns of your own show.

Chapter Seven
Our Mind, An Emotional Roller Coaster

"You cannot have a positive life and a negative mind."
Joyce Meyers

If we continually focus on the wrong things our mind can become our own worst enemy. The decisions we make are usually the result of our thoughts. We allow our thoughts to make decisions for us that are not always logical or in alignment with what we say we want for our lives.

When things don't work out the way we had hoped we start to live with a defeated mentality. Our mind will ensnare and trap us by either something we've gone through or by someone, even in our thought process, controlling and enslaving our life.

Deep down we may have already known that the guy who broke our heart or whom we finally parted ways wasn't the right one for us to begin with. But, we allowed our emotions to choose Mr. Wrong anyway.

We may have dreamed that he would be our version of Mr. Darcy from the film, Pride & Prejudice, adapted from the Jane Austen novel. Tall, handsome and wealthy, he was a sought after aristocratic bachelor who was smitten with an outspoken commoner named Lizzie.

But, in spite of their different backgrounds and the constant misunderstandings, he spent the next year correcting every wrong, that she pointed out, that stood between them and then asked for her hand in marriage.

When we enter a new relationship we want things to happen at lightening speed. We overlook incompatibility issues and ignore warning signs. Our intuition may be telling us, "this is all wrong, this guy is not right for you, he will break your heart." But we forge ahead anyway.

Looking back over my last serious relationship, I could see that my decision to get involved with Chris was not based on any logical reasoning. I had been single for over two years and during that entire time had my eye on a Physician's Assistant, whom Chris greatly resembled when I met him.

I had waited for my P.A. to make his move since I thought he felt the same way about me that I felt for him. But after two long, frustrating and agonizing years of waiting, I decided, reluctantly, it was time to move on. Perhaps I had misread how I thought he felt about me. And the thought that we would never be together was disheartening.

At the time I thought the only way to cure myself of him was to start dating someone else. But he was always there, in the back of my mind and I never stopped thinking about him.

But getting involved with someone who happens to resemble the one you love and wanted to be with isn't the wisest decision to make either and becomes a constant reminder of what could have been had you been given a chance.

The fact that Chris lived in the Midwest should have been enough to deter me from getting seriously involved as I really had no desire to enter into a long distance relationship.

Plus, he was a single father and I wasn't sure if I wanted to date someone divorced with young children but decided to take a chance anyway. After all, I thought to myself, "what did I have to lose?"

If I had a crystal ball at the time, I would have foreseen the outcome and would have never gotten into a relationship with him seeing that I ended up losing so much and paid the price financially long after the relationship was over.

The first couple of months I was swept off my feet by this man. I would awaken every morning to a text message from him, then a mid-morning call to see how my day was going, and then in the evening he would call me and we would talk for hours every single night until we both fell asleep.

When he finally came to see me a after a month of talking on the phone every day I felt like we already knew so much about each other. But the signs started surfacing when I met him in person and he slowly started to reveal things about himself that had never been discussed or brought up with me on the phone.

He would blurt out random things about his past relationships with women that should have prompted me to ask more questions which would be crucial to the events that eventually took place in our relationship. Instead, I ignored some of the things he said because those things happened in the past and didn't pertain to me, or so I thought.

After a wonderful two week visit, we had decided to date each other exclusively as he asked me, over breakfast, to be his girlfriend. But, within 24 hours after going back home to the Midwest he was back online. His profile had shown recently, "active". And, since he hadn't cancelled his membership I knew he had been actively looking for other women.

When he met me he decided to dump another girl he had been talking to that he met online but wasn't serious about because he was, supposedly, blown away by me. But the fact that he lied outright and said he hadn't been back on the dating site where we met was clearly another sign I should not have ignored.

I knew he was lying. Yet again, I brushed aside the warning signs and proceeded to get more deeply involved with him. He did eventually cancel his membership but he waited almost a month before doing so and I couldn't shake the uneasiness I was starting to feel. Lying about something like that meant that he would easily lie to me about other things.

Our thoughts are extremely powerful. And our intuition warns us when something doesn't feel right. We can count on them to guide us but our principles, values and standards need to be the deciding factor when we decide to partner with another person. And the only way to find out if are in alignment is to get to know them before diving deeper into unchartered waters.

We can ask God to give us the eyes of Christ, the discernment of the Holy Spirit and the heart of the Father when our minds are confused and we are unsure how to proceed with any uncertain situation that can change the course of our lives.

But when times get tough, during this period, and they will, it's easy to fall into a funk and become depressed or have a negative attitude toward life in general when things don't work out as we had hoped.

We go into a relationship with the best of intentions and when it falls apart we can really beat ourselves up over a failed relationship even if the fault wasn't completely our own.

When I get upset with myself for making bad decisions I am reminded of what Dr. John Maxwell said at another Sunday service. He stated, "that life is what happens to you while attitude is what you do with what happens to you."

And, the bible tells us to "fill our minds and meditate on the best, not the worst; the beautiful, not the ugly, things to praise, not things to curse." Philippians 4:8

But our mind will continue to dwell on what went wrong and replay painful scenes that won't allow us to close that chapter of our lives. Sometimes its easier just to allow ourselves to fall into a negative mindset.

Other times, we have all kinds of negative self talks. "I'll never find anyone else! Why did this have to happen to me? Why did God allow this to happen to me? I'm a good person, I didn't deserve this! I should be married already!" And on and on the negative thoughts flow.

Self pity might seem more comforting because right now the sun is shining just a little too brightly and all you want to do is draw the curtains and be left alone in your misery.

The deeper you fall into despair the harder it will be to pull yourself out of it. Find the strength and will to want to feel better. You're a beautiful person inside and out, created in the image and likeness of God. Take baby steps each day and make loving yourself a top priority. If God loves you then someone else will love you to.

My road, thus far, had been a rocky one. Although, I was able to transition into my new surroundings and settle in relatively quickly, I still faced many daunting challenges. I'd tried the online dating thing again and haven't made much success in the quality of men I was hoping to meet.

My stalker broke out my car window which cost me, out of pocket, almost $400.00 to fix during a time when I couldn't afford to pay for the replacement. My insurance wouldn't cover it because I had a $500 deductible.

But I had no choice. It was the dead of winter and thus far, the coldest, rainiest month I had encountered since moving to that area. So I had no choice but to take my meager savings and pay for a new window.

I'd been working two jobs six and sometimes seven days a week. One full time and the other one on weekends, leaving me little time for relaxation or a social life. And, in between, worked on writing my book and doing freelance copywriting projects when I could.

I continued struggling to make ends meet each month working two hourly jobs and knew that another change needed to be made if I wanted to improve the quality of my life again. I felt like I had gone backwards in life.

I would sometimes dwell on all I had given up, perhaps taken for granted. My high profile, high paying job and living in one of the most exclusive residences in West Palm Beach were all signs of my hard work and accomplishments. How could I have thrown it all away? And for someone whose promises amounted to nothing.

So, I could have easily fallen back into a negative mindset, and I sometimes did! But, when you find your thoughts shifting into the past or focusing on negative events, change the thought immediately by re-focusing your attention on something else. Read a good book or rent a movie you've been wanting to see. Anything that will take your mind off of your problems.

I have had friends who have gone through bad breakups and have either self medicated with prescription drugs or alcohol or they would go into overdrive and start partying like crazy to numb the pain they were feeling.

Sooner or later you are going to self-destruct with this type of behavior and eventually you will come off that high and will have to deal with those feelings you've been trying to mask. You need a good, solid base or foundation to lean on.

No matter how bad it gets, there is always hope. There is always a solution to every problem no matter how insurmountable the problem seems. During those times when I had fleeting moments of hopelessness and no one was around to offer comfort, I immediately, either listened to inspirational music, read some favorite scriptures or re-read highlighted passages from inspirational books.

Having a positive frame of mind and an optimistic outlook on life will result in a much happier life. Make it a point to not allow your mind to wander into negative thinking for long. Let your light shine and others will be drawn to your spirit.

Step 7:

ReFocus Your Mind On Whatever Is Lovely, True And Brings You Pleasure.

Keep a journal of your favorite verses, sayings, quotes, and scriptures. And, read them over and over again until you truly start to believe that they are life changing and your life will eventually transform for the better.

Chapter Eight
Theories & Reasonings

If you're like me, both a creative and intellectual thinker, who likes to analyze everything and then come up with theories and reasonings for why people do the things they do, you will drive yourself crazy, and completely exhaust yourself mentally in the process.

It will be impossible to move forward in a new relationship if we still live with a mindset that every action, reaction and nuance needs to be broken down and analyzed in parts.

Theories and reasonings cause so much confusion, doubt and fear as our mind works overtime trying to figure out why we were treated so badly in the first place. I think, as women, once we become suspicious, many of us start to look for the cause of our suspicions.

Near the end of my relationship, when the signs were so clear that something wasn't right, I was constantly looking for clues and signs that justified my train of thought that the man I was in a relationship with was cheating on me with others.

But, because of my line of questioning he became even better at covering his tracks. It became an obsession as I worked overtime trying to gain the proof that his shady behavior would prove he had been unfaithful.

I could have saved myself the trouble, anguish and aggravation as other parts of our relationship started unravelling, which in itself, were clear signs that something wasn't right. Whether I proved he was cheating or not, the fact that he was treating me badly and disrespectfully, should have been enough to end the relationship then and there.

His sudden lack of affection and interest in me, codes on his work and personal cell phone, unexplained day trips out of town, alone, on the only day we both had off to spend together, and his sudden flare ups when I asked questions he didn't like and wouldn't answer, were clear signs, in my opinion, that he was seeing someone else.

I told him that we should have no secrets from each other and should be totally transparent with one another, hiding nothing. He argued his right to privacy and said I had no business questioning him since he was an adult and could do whatever he wanted and accused me, again, of being insecure.

Although I respect a person's right to their own space and certainly don't need to be joined at the hip, I still believe that when you enter into a relationship with someone it should be open, upfront and honest. Otherwise, why bother going through the motions of pledging your love and devotion to each other?

Some of you may disagree and claim your right to privacy. But what happens when you're in the midst of a situation that may have you questioning your own relationship and your partner's suspicious behavior?

This is why it's so important at the beginning of a relation-ship to clearly state what's important to each of you and stand by what you believe in. We can easily lose sight of who we are and what we stand for in the early stages of love. We don't want anything interfering with those feelings of euphoria.

Although, in the beginning, as Chris and I were getting to know each other we talked at length about what was important to each of us such as being honest and faithful and communi-cating our needs to one another. However, this quickly wore off within the first year of the relationship.

When we're with the wrong person we have to work espe-cially hard to get the other person to behave in a manner that we think is appropriate or will make us happy. We bend over backwards, forwards and do cartwheels to hopefully, get them to do what we want.

This isn't normal behavior. If you're with someone with whom you are compatible you will both respect each other's differences yet love each other enough that you won't even need to ques-tion what the other person is doing when they're not with you. Because you will not give each other a reason to be distrustful.

I'm all for a guy having a night out with his buddies. But, when he's getting dressed up, grooming himself carefully and asking me to shave his back, he isn't going to go and hang out with his buddies.

If communication shuts down, and he claims nothing is wrong, when its apparent that something isn't right, this is when we start forming theories about his odd behavior. And, the same goes for when he's being overly nice and presenting you with an expensive gift out of the blue when it's not his character.

Some of you may not even want to address these theories and just continue day in and day out as if nothing is wrong. I know women who had proof that their partner was cheating on them yet, they chose to do nothing about it as long as he came home to them at night and they didn't have to be alone.

One thing I learned about being in a relationship is that you can still feel lonely living in the same household. This is especially true if you have no other interests outside of his and you're being ignored and shut out.

Couples sometimes stay together for convenience while leading separate lives. I could never do that. Even when I told Chris I was leaving he asked me to stay and continue to split the bills with him while assuming we would see other people. There was no way I was going to agree to such a ridiculous agreement.

Joyce Meyer stated that "reasoning occurs when a person tries to figure out the "why" behind something. Reasoning causes the mind to revolve around and around a situation, issue, or event attempting to understand all its intricate component parts."

Imagine going through life trying to figure out why friends and ex-boyfriends hurt you, betrayed you, turned their back on you, lied to you, and cheated on you. You become mentally exhausted in this wretched state and will never have peace of mind.

I used to tell myself that I will refute arguments and theories and reasonings and every proud and lofty thing that sets itself up against the true knowledge of God, hoping to calm myself down while continuing to try and figure out what was going on.

I even went into therapy and tried to get Chris to go with me but he refused. He thought it was a great idea that I go since I was clearly the problem and he didn't have any issues at least that's what he thought.

The therapy did not make me feel any better it just made me realize the problems were never going to go away, clearly a sign that our relationship had run its course.

I thought back to my previous, long term relationship of thirteen years. None of the issues that I had experienced with Chris were ever a problem. Mark had been open and honest with me. He never tried to hide anything from me, didn't put codes on his phone or act in any manner that made me suspicious of him.

To this day, we are still really good friends and I will always love him. He never got into another serious relationship after me and that has to say a lot about how much he loved me because he never found anyone else that he thought could replace me. Although, if he does eventually find someone I will be very happy for him.

As I continue to learn from my mistakes I have reasoned that if God wanted me to know everything then I would. We will never get all of our questions answered about why others treated us so badly. And, honestly, what others think about us is really none of our business anyway.

When we learn to let go of this damaging thought process it really does free our mind to work on things that really matter. Had I not cleared my mind of the garbage and clutter that were filling it then I wouldn't have had the creative thoughts in place to even write this book you are now reading.

When my mind was clouded with negative thoughts I couldn't put pen to paper. I had complete writers block. The creativity wasn't there and I walked around angry, upset and unhappy.

When you allow good thoughts to flow through you and free your mind of the heavy burdens that weigh you down you can feel free to enjoy the things that make you happy and bring you joy.

If you're a person who loves being in a relationship and have been in a long, extended one, and now you find yourself suddenly single, the journey won't be an easy one. But there will be days where you think, "I can do this!"

And other days, something may trigger a negative thought that you are indeed single on those nights you would love to go out on a date or snuggle with someone while you watch a movie and eat popcorn.

There will be days where you feel excluded as if no one cares about you, and wonder if you will ever meet anyone again and if there are even any normal guys out there that also happen to be available and attractive. I know because I still struggle with these thoughts myself. But don't let them consume you.

Keep an open mind when you finally do meet someone new but also listen to your intuition and any warning signs that may be cause for alarm. In the beginning, try not to form opinions or theories and just observe the other person's behavior and see if their words mesh with their actions.

I remember Chris had flown into town for my forty-third birthday. We had only been dating for two months and I wanted us to go to one of the amusement parks in Orlando for the day.

It started out as a great day but when we left the park and were walking through the parking lot he kept checking out a woman that was with someone else. I remember he couldn't take his eyes off of her and it was upsetting to me but I said nothing.

From that point on whenever we were out and about I would notice him checking out other women and trying to make eye contact with them. At some point I calmly explained how upsetting this was to me when he did this and how disrespectful it was to me especially when we were together. But, of course, he denied doing this.

Sometimes I would see the women looking at me with a puzzled look on their faces. I could only imagine what they might have been thinking. "If this guy is with her why is he flirting with me?" Some women, having no class, would flirt right back with him in front of me. I often reasoned that if he was doing this in my presence then what was he doing when I wasn't around?

And, if he hoped one of these women would call him but he couldn't give out his number in front of me, that wasn't a problem either. He had his phone number plastered all over his truck and all he had to do was drive slowly away so they had a clear picture of his number and could write it down.

And, although that was also the way he advertised his business, in my opinion, I believe it was a way for him to pick up women. He even had his personal number on the back of his boat. I thought this was just another way to get attention.

The warning signs I received so early in our relationship couldn't have been any clearer as to what lay ahead for me if I continued with this relationship. But I forged ahead anyway hoping these were just innocent flirtations. My thoughts didn't bring me any peace of mind and would cause major problems between us as time went on.

So choose wisely and ask yourself the important questions when you meet someone for the first time. Are their values in alignment with your own? If they have young children are you prepared to become a new step mother?

Does he have a roving eye and constantly checking out and flirting with other women in your presence? Have you caught him lying and changing his stories or blaming his ex-wife for everything that went wrong in their relationship?

And, are you already forming theories and reasonings as the relationship progresses as you catch him lying and your mind races to process inaccuracies in his stories but you brush off your theories anyway?

Either give yourself some space to figure out if you should proceed with this relationship or continue to date other people until you find a connection with someone that doesn't have you doubting or questioning his motives.

You will know when "the right one" comes along. The relationship will feel like a breath of fresh air and you won't have doubts and fears about him and his intentions toward you.

He will be consistent in word and action and show his love and devotion toward you. He will respectfully refrain from checking out other women in your presence and not give you cause to question his behavior.

Step 8:

We will never fully understand why others hurt us or constantly disappointed us.

So, how can we move forward in our lives knowing these relationships will never be mended? How can you take the pain of your past and use it for your good going forward? What steps can you take to protect yourself when meeting a potential mate and making new friends?

Chapter Nine
A Loveless Culture

How many people are out there still searching for love? Why are there so many lonely people in the world when we live in a country inhabited by millions? Could it be that we have simply lost faith in man?

And, how is that when Mother Teresa was alive, having visited many countries, she observed and commented that America was the most loveless country she had ever visited?

What's happened to our culture that we live in a society of cold-hearted and selfish, people? I've even noticed it in some of the churches I have attended which is even worse, because as Christians, we should be leading by example.

It doesn't take much effort to show kindness to strangers or be open to receiving new people into your closed inner circles. Even as adults we form "cliques" and rarely make room to allow others into our lives.

Then there are those so desperate to be a part of the crowd they don't even stand up for what they believe in anymore and will fall for anything as long as they are part of the majority, even if that means compromising their own morals and values.

We have all experienced, at one time or another, in our lives, feelings of abandonment and of not feeling loved. From the time I was a young girl, in middle school, I remember being beaten and abused by my step-father who would then tell my mother to give me up for adoption.

I could never figure out why this man hated me so much since I wasn't a bad kid, I just wasn't his kid. He would wait until my mum left for work and then come charging into my room telling me to take my clothes off. When I refused he would beat me while my two step-sisters hid in their bedrooms. He never touched them.

When he broke my arm and my mother had to take me to the emergency room she begged me to lie to the doctors and say I fell while playing outside so he wouldn't go to jail and get kicked out of the military. So, I lied as my mother instructed.

The night he placed a butcher knife under the bed he shared with my mum who found it when she dropped something on the floor was the night he had planned on killing her when she went to sleep and probably me as well.

She quietly went into the bathroom, ran her nightly bath water as she normally did, while Mr. Evil sat downstairs watching T.V. I was in my room doing homework as were my step-sisters.

Thank God there was a window in that bathroom that led out to a slanted roof. My mother pretended to take a bath and proceeded to escape out the 2nd floor bathroom window and worked her way down the drain pipe on the side of the house and ran to a neighbors to call the police.

He was arrested within the hour and that gave my mother the courage to leave him for good. Because of his high rank in the military, he was able to get all charges dropped with just a slap on the wrist but he was out of our lives for good and for that I was grateful.

Just a few years ago, I experienced, yet again, just how cruel people can be while living in South Florida. After I parted ways with my boyfriend of thirteen years, I was maneuvering the dating world as a single woman and enjoying my freedom. But, I became a pawn in a sick game being played against me in the small community where I had lived.

For the first time, I saw how shallow people could be as I was judged based on my outer appearance. Funny, how none of this was even a thought when I was in a relationship. But, I remember one incident that took place at my local gym that caused me to feel self conscious about my body for years.

A well known Surgeon proceeded to tell the guy I had a huge crush on, who happened to be the Physician Assistant, that I mentioned in an earlier chapter, that he noticed that my body was flabby as he walked by and saw me running on the treadmill.

At the time, I had been heavier and had started losing weight and getting toned up. I was going through a transformation and doing it the proper way which included cardio and strength training and took time, meaning it wasn't happening overnight. But, I was horrified when this doctor told my crush this news right before my eyes.

Things got so bad at that particular gym that I ended up canceling my gym membership and driving further away to another gym so I could work out without being constantly judged and put down.

These were childish, pathetic games being played by grown professional people. After seven months away from my original gym, I decided to go back. After all, it was right across the street from where I lived and I had acquired more self confidence in myself and my body.

I had lost all of my excess weight and was much firmer and more toned. The Surgeon was in shock when he saw me, it was apparent from his expression. I had lost the weight and toned up without resorting to plastic surgery which I couldn't afford anyway.

I was complimented and congratulated on how I looked but I never forget how I had been treated before, by these same people, when I was heavier and I remained cautious around them.

I learned quickly that our culture celebrates one's physical form over any other qualities. And when a person finally starts to look good these same people will strip you down from head to toe to find something negative to talk about while at the same time complimenting you for turning into a beautiful swan.

Even as women, we tend to put each other down to our friends so we can feel better about ourselves. Some may think nothing of sneaking behind a friend's back to sleep with their man or flirt shamelessly with him because of wanting what they have.

I've gotten anonymous text messages calling me fat bitch in the past and God knows what else has been said behind my back but I've learned to ignore the haters. I'm not an ugly woman by any means and certainly don't consider myself fat but I've sure been made to feel ugly by others' ugly words.

Growing up I had always dreamed of being a high fashion model, walking the runways of Paris and gracing magazine covers. And for many years I worked in the fashion industry and attended meetings in many designer showrooms as a sales consultant.

After seeing fit models draped in a perfect sample size 6 and attending photo shoots that involved 6ft. tall fashion models I quickly came back to reality. I was neither tall nor rail thin but was always told by strangers walking the streets of Manhattan that I should be modeling.

At the time, I admired theses women who were obviously blessed with the exact body types the industry demanded. No petite, curvy women were allowed back then. And, I don't think much has changed today in that respect.

As I grew wiser and more comfortable in my own skin I saw how so many young girls look up to and idolize celebrities. Even some adults have had surgery to alter their appearance to resemble their favorite stars which I find disturbing.

We can admire someone without idolizing them or trying to alter our appearance to look more like them and less like ourselves. I want to cringe every time I hear someone on TV saying that "so and so is my idol." Really?

How about making Jesus Christ your idol? At least he can offer you salvation and eternal life. Can we come up with another word to describe admiration for someone other than "idol"?

Not only do we celebrate physical beauty but we are overly impressed by how popular a certain person may be with others. You may have a personal Facebook page with over 500 "friends" but how many of them would come to your rescue if you were in dire straights and needed help?

In our shallow self-entitled world many are not willing to make that kind of sacrifice for another human being. We say we want to be loved but then push the person away and treat them like crap when they give us the very thing we so desperately crave.

Some may even see love as a sign of weakness and the weak are usually the ones used, abused and walked all over. But, we must not give up hope. Don't let the world bury your light or your willingness to love others regardless of their faults. Because we all have them, some people just ignore their own, by magnifying others to take the focus off their own shortcomings.

In the midst of trying to live and love in a world that doesn't want to love us back, we have to stand firm and strong against such overwhelmingly negative forces. When we're made fun of, pushed away, betrayed, used or abused, we must find the strength within ourselves to keep on loving anyway.

Think of the betrayal, abuse and horrible death that Jesus suffered for the sake of our sins. Yet, when he was nailed to the cross, he didn't curse his enemies but instead said, "forgive them father, for they know not what they do."

No matter how badly we've been beaten down by another's words if we say we want love in our lives and to be loved then we have to be willing to forgive others. We can't possibly move on and be prosperous in a new relationship if were still harboring bitterness and anger in our hearts toward the person who betrayed us.

If someone chooses to play games with you, at your expense, that doesn't mean you need to be a willing participant. Ignore them. And, yes, (sigh) grown men and women are still playing games with each other!

If someone chooses not to be your friend anymore then bless and release them. Why waste precious energy on people whose behavior you can't control anyway?Life doesn't stand still for anyone and it's not worth your time bending over backwards trying to get someone to like you or forgive you for some insignificant or imagined wrong.

Keep moving forward and if that person is meant to be a part of your life's journey then they will join you again when the time is right. Life doesn't offer any guarantees either so don't put your life on hold for someone else unless they are fully committed to you. Fully embrace the reality of the situation now and not the ideal of the relationship and what you're hoping for in the future.

It's no secret that I'm a romantic at heart. I do want to be swept off my feet by the man of my dreams and I have a very clear picture of what he might look like as we have all pictured, at one time or another, the person we thought we might marry and spend our lives with.

I can picture my wedding day wearing a long flowing silk dress with a wreath of flowers in my long wavy hair, walking barefoot, with my now five year old niece as the flower girl. And, there he would stand gazing at me with such love, devotion and desire in his eyes.

As I approach him we can't take our eyes off each other. We have both waited for this moment for so long. He towers over my 5"4 frame. And as he pulls me in toward him, to kiss me deeply, a warmth courses through my body and I feel like I'm going to faint. He pulls me closer, still, and I wrap my arms around his neck touching him, as if for the first time, as my fingertips brush across his skin.

Now can you imagine the outcome had I been carrying bitterness and anger in my heart? My entire demeanor would be different. My aura would not shine brightly and the energy between the two of us wouldn't be as magnetic had it been the real thing.

Had I carried around un-forgiveness in my heart we would have started our married lives together with very real problems if we had even gotten that far. But by forgiving, you can walk into a new relationship with a new partner and a clean slate. The past is behind you so why drag it into the present and the future?

Yes, we live in a loveless, selfish culture. But whose fault is that? As parents are we teaching both our sons and daughters how to be respectful and loving toward others? Do you show them love and tell them how much you love them? Or push them away?

Do you teach them right from wrong or allow them to dis-respect you while treating them like a BFF? And, give them everything they want out of guilt for not spending enough time with them or because they have made you feel as if they are somehow, self entitled?

They learn by example and if you don't provide guidance they're left to look for it in all the wrong places. And what about the culture of our schools? Why aren't there more programs that teach social skills and etiquette?

We spend so much time on the internet and texting that many don't even know how to have a meaningful, face to face, conversation anymore. And, remember hand written love letters?

One actually picked up pen and paper and wrote a personal heartfelt letter. Sadly, those have been replaced with text messages where the meaning is often misinterpreted.

I watched a documentary recently where the narrator held up a picture of Jesus and asked a room full of kids if they knew who he was. One kid said Abraham Lincoln, another Ronald McDonald and a third George Washington. Many just shrugged and stated they didn't know.

Yet, hold up a picture of the most popular pop star of the moment and most of the kids in the room would know who that person is and could probably even sing you a few of his or her songs.

Then there's job culture. We live in a time where arrogance and greed and corporate culture dominate certain industries. I've heard stories of people fighting to get ahead in the workforce, stabbing each other in the back, or promoting their friends who have no experience for the job while turning their back on those that do simply because they can.

Instead of taking a job just because you need a paycheck make sure the company culture is in alignment with your values. Check to see if management shows a genuine interest in their employees and their wellbeing and offers incentives that are fair and achievable.

There are those who abuse their power and authority instead of using it in a manner that will make a positive impact on the lives of others. And the overly self righteous who walk around like they have never committed a sin who are quick to point the finger at someone else who has done wrong.

We are only human. We make mistakes and should be forgiven for them. I love the line Jesus speaks in the movie, Jesus Of Nazareth, when he says, "let he who is without sin cast the first stone." Jesus forgave us yet we expect others to be judged and punished harshly. And when the tables are turned, we demand forgiveness and mercy.

And when we feel like justice hasn't been served we then become judge and jury and want to take matters into our own hands and exact punishment on others who we feel deserve what they get.

It isn't easy letting go of the hurt and anger we feel towards someone who has wronged us and we can harbor these bitter emotions for years to come. But what good will that do us? By letting these emotions control us we allow ourselves to still be chained to the that person and the past.

How many of you have friends that came into your life and things seemed to be going well and then all of a sudden they stopped communicating with you for no apparent reason?

When they don't return your phone calls or text messages you rack your brain trying to figure out what you could have done to piss them off. In this instance you can't even ask for forgiveness because you have no idea what you did wrong.

Even promising or long term friendships are apparently, easily disposable. It's easier to have no friends at all or quickly make another disposable friend than to salvage a friendship that can never be replaced. And, relationships are no different.

There will never be perfect conditions to fall in love and be together. Men are especially prone to making excuses when it comes to committing to a relationship even if they know, in their heart, the person is right for them.

They use any and every excuse in the book. They may say, "My job comes first. I have to wait until I pay off my student loans from ten years ago. I'm not ready for her yet. I work fifty hours a week, how can I make time for a relationship?" Or, "She could definitely be the one, but what if there's someone out there that I might like better in the future?"

If you're going to spend your life with someone they are going to be a part of all aspects of your life, both the good and the bad. That's why in a marriage it says, "for better or for worse". It is understood, by both parties, that things won't be perfect and you will love and accept them regardless of the circumstances.

Looking for the perfect mate under perfect conditions is as unrealistic as expecting a knight in shining armor to show up on horseback and sweep you off your feet. So, when it comes to love, take your cues from Jesus, not the world. He loves us unconditionally with all of our flaws and imperfections.

There is a natural order to life and the right person will be drawn to you for exactly the right reasons. They may not even be able to describe how or why but know that they love you, flaws and all.

Before this book even became an idea, I sent the following message to a small group of my friends that sums up this chapter perfectly:

"Have we become so shallow that we don't even consider the person in their entirety but only by the sum of their body parts? If you love someone, instead of finding fault, build them up. Help them achieve their potential and greatness and, in doing so, you achieve your own.

And don't just discard or disregard someone because they don't meet 100% of your standards. You may be passing up the best thing that could ever happen to you had you given that person a chance.

Chasing the perfect 10 will never fulfill you and make you happy because the perfect 10 doesn't exist. And, if you're only judging the person by their outer appearance then sadly, you've lost the meaning of this entire message.

Any ordinary person can find fault with another and tear them down but it takes an extraordinary person to say, "the hell with all that, you're amazing just the way you are."

And that's what love is all about.

Step 9:

How Can You Show More Love To Others?

What can you do to show that love? It's not enough to just say it. What actions can you take, if you're in a position to do so, to help someone out in need?

Think of someone you know that you could offer your help or contacts to get a business started or recommend them for a better paying job that you know they qualify for.

Part 2

New

Beginnings

Chapter Ten
Learning To Love Yourself

Practicing self love can be difficult especially if you were in a relationship where you were constantly put down or made to feel unloved. You may perceive yourself as not good enough or worthy of finding anyone who will treat you the way you deserve to be treated. You may even put yourself down and obsess over or magnify your flaws.

I realized recently that I was constantly putting myself down. This was something I had done for years. I became my own worst enemy as I stood in the mirror and obsessed over every little flaw and how a potential partner might perceive these flaws.

Once I decided that there were worst things in the world to be concerned about such as starving children, the homeless, and friends and family members fighting life threatening illnesses, I realized how shallow and pathetic I was to be concerned about how someone else was perceiving the way I looked.

I reasoned that if we could all just see ourselves the way God sees us then we wouldn't spend time tearing ourselves down or trying to make ourselves feel better by putting someone else down for the way they look.

Years of bad habits don't just undo themselves overnight so when I find myself scrutinizing my appearance I remind myself that only men look at the outer appearance, and judge accordingly, but God looks at the internal, what is in our hearts.

We have to stop judging each other just because we don't look a certain way and look at the person as a whole. What good is it if they look like perfection but then have an ugly personality. Someone overweight could have a thyroid problem or may have had to take steroids for an illness that made her gain weight. A very thin, emaciated woman may have an eating disorder causing her both emotional and psychological problems.

As women we constantly size each other up, compete for the same men and assume we are better looking than the other because we have a nicer body and look better in a bathing suit. Men can be just as shallow in their assessment of women.

No wonder so many couples become disillusioned with each other. When we decide to partner with someone based on such shallow requirements how could any relationship withstand actual problems?

When we start loving ourselves completely we stop choosing people who we believe will validate our self worth. As long as you look for someone else to make you feel good about yourself you will always be miserable. And, I find the more beautiful you are perceived to be the more people tend to look for flaws and want to tear you down.

Loving yourself means loving every part of you. Sure, there are areas of our body we may not be happy with and obsess over, declaring, "if only I didn't have stretch marks or cellulite then I would be happy and could have any guy I want."

If a guy can't love you because you have imperfections or because your imperfections turn him off please run to the nearest exit. You don't want to be with someone like that anyway.

First of all, even if that wasn't a problem or you could get those areas fixed through some sort of plastic surgery procedures, he would still find other things that turn him off about you.

There are men out there who will fall in love with you even if you were missing a limb so those are the type of guys you want to spend your life with. Not, Shallow Hal. You don't want to be with someone who will put you down and make you feel worse about yourself.

Now that you're single, this isn't the time to start letting yourself go by binge eating and not taking care of yourself either. It will only make you feel worse and your self esteem will take an even bigger nose dive.

Take care of yourself by eating right and working out. Your body will love you for it. You will have more energy, feel confident and sexier as your body becomes more shapely and toned.

People who haven't met us and don't know what we look like may assume that as a single woman in our forties we must look like middle aged, unkempt women with five cats to keep us company.

I'm not knocking anyone who happens to own cats, I'm actually allergic to them and can't have one, but it is one description that has stigmatized women in our age group.

It's all in how you carry yourself, how you dress, how you style your hair and makeup and how you take care of your body. Some of you may be "old souls" and come across more mature for your age and that's fine, if it makes you feel good about yourself.

Others, such as myself are "young souls" and probably look and appear much younger than how a typical forty something woman would be perceived. And, we don't always act our age which is probably what helps keep us young and youthful looking. Let's be clear here, feeling young isn't the same thing as acting immature.

I like to wear my hair long and loose and don't have gray hair that needs to be colored every four weeks. I'm lucky in that I don't have to have Botox to smooth out wrinkles because of my Indian, Spanish and German heritage. My skin doesn't age as quickly.

We are each unique in that we all have genes that lend themselves to something wonderful and beautiful that makes us stand out and has the opposite sex taking notice. So, embrace and enhance what you can and don't obsess over what you can't and have no control over.

Being in our forties is challenging in more ways than just being single. For one, our metabolism may start to slow down. It's harder to lose fat while fighting to maintain muscle tone. Some, may already be going through menopause.

Then there is the fight to keep wrinkles away, banish belly fat, smooth out cellulite on hips, thighs and buttocks, deal with thinning dry hair, sagging breasts or droopy bottoms and the list can go on and on causing even more frustration and self esteem issues.

Not all of us will have all of these issues to deal with and some of us may only deal with one or two of them but that doesn't mean we won't magnify and focus on those one or two areas that drive us crazy.

It can be hard work keeping in shape and looking great. But loving yourself means not giving up on looking your best. If you're allowing yourself to go downhill then you are not loving yourself and trust me, if you don't, no one else will either.

Your break up may have been a relief or it may have been incredibly painful but know that you are loved and are lovable and the right one will come along and capture your heart.

It takes effort to look and feel good about ourselves when we're feeling sad and depressed or unworthy. But I promise you by making an effort your self confidence will start to soar and your mood will become more elevated.

During this life transition and transformation we not only want to work on our outer appearance but our inner selves as well. There is no point in making ourselves look amazing on the outside while walking around harboring bitterness and anger on the inside. You have to let all of that go.

Do whatever it takes to make you feel good mentally and emotionally whether that involves meditation, yoga, Pilates, going to church or walks on the beach. It's important to keep a positive mindset and to focus on things that bring joy to your heart, mind, body and soul.

How is it that we can easily give our love to another yet not practice loving ourselves more? When we practice self-love we are not willing to allow ourselves to be treated disrespectfully.

A close friend of mine admitted that when she feels lonely she engages in sexual encounters with various men, some are even married. I asked her if she felt less lonely after her sexual escapades and she admitted that she felt worse. She would continue this vicious cycle trying to rid herself of feelings of loneliness, yet, causing her sense of self worth to plummet at the same time.

She is an upbeat, attractive woman in her forties who is going through a divorce and has done well for herself by establishing a new business and buying herself a nice home. Yet, she doesn't feel comfortable being alone after living in a home with her husband and college age kids. It depresses her and so she seeks intimacy from whomever she can.

Every individual is different and each of us knows what makes us feel good and what will make us feel awful about ourselves. I don't judge this friend for the decisions she makes but I also know that I couldn't engage in casual sex or have a friend with benefits. I prefer to go without and save myself for a serious relationship.

I'm a romantic at heart and prefer to be wooed in the beginning of a relationship. I like getting to know a person with the anticipation of whats to come once we become intimate.

As a woman, I give of myself fully and completely to the person I'm in a relationship with so having random sexual encounters would leave me feeling used and empty.

I know some women, especially if their partners have neglected them or make them feel unattractive, may enter into a relationship with an unavailable man. Others may have self esteem issues and also choose men who cannot offer them anything more than a few random sexual encounters.

But how does that make you feel afterwards? When he goes home to be with his wife or partner and you're left alone again? What about holidays and special occasions? He could never spend those with you if he has a family at home.

I am reminded of another friend who was having an affair with her boss. He was married with two young children and she a single mother to a young beautiful daughter. They worked closely together all day and would have sexual encounters whenever and wherever they could.

Sometimes he would sneak her over to his home when his wife was out shopping for a few hours or off visiting her mum with their children. They would have sex in his bed that he shared with his wife and in various places throughout his home.

I was terrified for my girlfriend that his wife was going to come home early and find them out and yet shocked that this man's wife hadn't suspected that her husband was cheating on her with his co-worker. I thought, "how could she be so naive?"

My girlfriend was on cloud nine when they were together. But, when there was a long weekend or holiday that came around and he spent that time with his family, she was miserable. He talked about leaving his wife, so she claimed, once the children were older, and sadly, she decided to wait for him.

Her daughter had learned of the affair and we begged her to go out and meet someone that was available, someone she didn't have to sneak around with behind closed doors but she refused.

She was madly in love with this man. She would do things with him that his wife wouldn't do and felt as if she had some power over him that his wife did not. She was already in her late thirties, a single mother, who was going to put her future on hold for a promise that might never happen.

Each person chooses their own path in life and only you know what your tolerance levels are. Ultimately, loving yourself will involve doing what makes you happy but it shouldn't be at the expense of another person.

In choosing to love every aspect of yourself, you will be more inclined to choose a man that is not only available but won't have someone else standing in the way of loving you fully and completely.

Step 10:

What Changes Can You Make To Love Yourself More?

Write down things that bring you personal fulfillment and joy. Perhaps a day at the spa getting a massage and facial? If you had relationships in the past with unavailable men why do you think you chose those types of men? How did those encounters make you feel afterwards? What changes can you make now that will help you make different choices in the future?

Chapter Eleven
Not All Men Are Relationship Material

It can be difficult to get some men to connect and focus on a much deeper emotional level with one person especially if they have gone most of their life without having any meaningful or long term relationships.

Why is this? Probably because at some point in their past someone hurt them deeply and they vowed never to allow themselves to get that emotionally involved ever again with anyone. As women we pick up on this type of behavior in certain men but pursue them anyway thinking it will be different with us.

It takes time getting to know someone you plan on giving your heart to again. A few months doesn't mean you know everything about this person. You only know what they have told you but now you need to see for yourself, as a relationship progresses, who this person is by the way they interact with you and others.

By being fully present and attuned to another person requires good listening skills. People don't really listen to each other anymore and can misinterpret what the other person is saying and totally miss out on important clues as to whom that person really is verses who they want you to believe they are.

Being socially connected with another can grow into a deeper bond by allowing you to lose yourself and let go during intimacy and lovemaking. Men who have sex with random women rarely form a deep connection with them making it easy for them to have casual sex and move on to their next conquest.

But, even if you're a great listener and a great communicator and connect with someone on an emotional level, if you ignore the warning signs that go against your values or what you want in a relationship, you are in for a rocky road and a disappointing ending.

The guy who says he wants to be in a relationship but doesn't want marriage or children probably means it. But the woman who is looking for both marriage and children probably should look for someone whose values match her own. Many times women think they can change a man once they get into a relationship with him. It rarely works out that way.

You will exhaust yourself trying to change someone's views and character traits which only leads to frustration. It really isn't worth the effort unless one or the other is willing to compromise.

Men will give you clues as to how they feel about women in general and their past relationships with them. But you need to listen carefully during this interchange and ask questions if something is bothering you.

From my experience the guy whose answer is, "it's complicated", without offering any further explanation is either hiding something or still involved with someone else and you should proceed with caution if you decide to proceed at all.

At this stage of our lives we don't want to waste anymore time on men who close themselves off emotionally or otherwise. A relationship cannot be built on lies, deception and secrets.

Our job isn't to figure men out, attempt to fix them, mold them or scold them. They shouldn't be a science project that we have to work on improving but an equal partner who takes full responsibility and accountability for his part in the relationship.

Our goal, especially, in the crucial first stages of a relationship, should be to find out if we're compatible, can tolerate each other's differences, be open-minded and nonjudgmental toward their past, forgiving of our own and be clear on what we want from each other.

If you happen to meet a wonderful man who wants to take care of you and protect you all the days of your life it's still a good idea to be able to support yourself should things not work out as originally planned. Some men may become extremely controlling if you are too dependent on them.

I think most men find women more desirable when they've got their own thing going on unless they're insecure or feel threatened by your independence. I've personally found that some men feel uncomfortable around an extremely talented and accomplished woman.

If I were writing an online dating profile it might read something like this: I grew up in the Middle East and Europe, was an opera singer and belly dancer. I co-formed a band called The Faithful and we created a contemporary christian cd, called Bearing Good Fruit, that received radio airplay overseas. I love riding sport motorcycles and accomplished at horseback riding. I'm also a writer and published author.

Sadly, some guys may read that type of profile and think it's to good to be true! Then, why is she single? Something must be wrong with her. A few may feel intimidated and pass altogether. And, then their are the guys that feel the need to compete instead of just appreciating being with a woman who has so much to offer.

We all have hobbies, skills and accomplishments that make us interesting to the opposite sex. My advice is just don't throw them all out there at him, at once. Gradually reveal things about yourself leaving a bit of mystery and in the process not overwhelming him.

While you don't want to play down your accomplishments a man may feel like you don't need him if you can do everything yourself. Men want an independent woman yet, want to feel needed. So, I have learned not to disclose all of my abilities or capabilities until I get to know someone.

Men want a woman who isn't clingy, yet, they want your full attention. They may crave their freedom yet, secretly enjoy having you around and the security of the relationship. They may even come across as unemotional, but deep down inside, have a heart that cares.

They may look at other women but desire only to be with you. They may not show their feelings often but their eyes say it all. They may not be effective communicators, but remember the small details that make all the difference when it comes to loving you.

Be the confident, sexy, independent and level headed woman that shows you've got it all together even if you don't. Don' t play the helpless victim or complain about how bad you've got it now that you no longer have anyone around to mow the grass or take your car in for oil changes or repairs.

For some of you this may cause you to feel overwhelmed and you may have the need to rush into another relationship before you're ready. I know how tough it can be as I've experienced these same thoughts myself.

But don't allow your emotions to get the best of you and make you feel incompetent or incapable of taking care of yourself. Remember, even during your times of weakness, you're still a strong, independent woman who can take care of your own needs.

When it comes to men they may not necessarily be gifted at discerning our needs, wants and desires but they can definitely tell if you're coming across as desperate, needy or insecure in who you are as a person.

I was able to learn firsthand what my "crush" thought of me when one of his friends alerted me to a quote he had put on his Facebook page that said, "if she's easy, she won't be amazing and if she's amazing, she won't be easy. Yep, she's amazing, and I"m not worthy."

Here's a guy that I'd wanted to be with for several years, and he knew it. Yet, at the time, he would never approach me because HE didn't feel worthy. As a Physician's Assistant, practically a Doctor, educated, good looking and popular with both sexes, he didn't think he was worthy of me.

I felt helpless and sad when I read what he posted to his wall on Facebook because I knew there wasn't much I could do to make him feel worthy if he had it in his mind that he wasn't.

Men tend to exceed incredibly well in their work environ-ment, but when it comes to relationships and love, some men seem incapable of expressing it in ways that we need to see and hear or give us the attention we deserve.

Let's review some of the most common types of men we may be drawn to so we don't waste precious time, in the future, continually chasing the wrong types.

The "Shallow Hal" type of guy may be in his late thirties or forties, is picky and has plenty of his own insecurities but he masks them by spending all his time tearing down a woman because of her flaws, no matter how minute they may be.

He may be looking for a twenty something that he has nothing in common with but he needs to feed his ego as he imagines being envied for having a hot young thing by his side, when all he looks, is well, pathetic. He will then complain, once again, how he can't find a good woman.

He may have learned his lesson with chasing younger women and may give you a shot but you had better look much younger than your age and have a perfect body to get his attention otherwise, he will magnify every single one of your flaws and dump you when he thinks he has found someone more visually appealing.

Next, there's "Mr. Perfect". Similar to Shallow Hal but more sophisticated, he never has a hair out of place and you will never see him sweat or doing anything domesticated like mowing the lawn or getting himself dirty doing car repairs.

Someone must have told him that he was Mr. Flawless and he believed it and is stuck on himself. He will pick a woman apart for her flaws and use every excuse to break off a promising relationship because he doesn't like something about her that is probably insignificant, but a turn off to him because that is all he can focus on.

The woman on his arm must be eye candy from head to toe regardless of her IQ. This is the type of guy who will consider a woman with a perfect physique "talented" over a woman who actually has talent. And not that a woman with a perfect body can't be talented as well but this type isn't looking for the smartest woman in the room.

Some of these types will deliberately choose women who are not as attractive as they are because they want all the attention focused on them and their good looks.

He will make you feel insecure about yourself or put you down or worse, compare you to other women that, in his mind, he thinks are more attractive. He will set unrealistic expectations and expect you to achieve them at your own expense.

He will rarely compliment you because he's too busy admiring himself. He will constantly tell you how lucky you are to have a "catch" like him while running around cheating on you with other women because he craves the excitement and instant gratification of these meaningless one night stands.

And in his misguided mind he needs this attention to validate his self worth by sleeping with as many willing participants as possible. The more women he sleeps with the more popular and loved he perceives himself to be.

And, he will make no apologies for his damaging behavior because after all he can have any woman he wants. You don't like it? He will show you the door and won't give you a second thought since he has no problem finding his next conquest.

"The Coward" is the type of guy who allows his friend's to do all his thinking for him. If all he can talk about is you with his friends and they sense he is falling for you they may do whatever they can to prevent this from happening.

They will try and find fault with you physically or they will parade other women in his face in the hopes that he won't settle for you because he is, after all, a guy and isn't supposed to fall so hard for one woman.

His single friends will insist "bros before hoes" and lay a guilt trip on him about all the time he might be spending with you. His married friends will tell him all the reasons why he should remain single for as long as possible even into rocking chair age.

They will nitpick everything about you and tell him you're not right for him because you're to fat, to thin, to tall, to short, not the right nationality or whatever else they can think of to discourage him from being with you.

He will become so confused by all this bad advice he will end up pulling away from you and basically drifting into oblivion while you're left with a broken heart wondering what happened and why he left when you both knew you were perfect for each other.

Unless the coward learns to stand up to his family and friends he will miss out on the woman of his dreams. And, if he truly is not man enough to stand up to them and wants to be with you then he may have to make a drastic change and pick up and move to another part of the state, with you, if necessary so your relationship has a fighting chance.

But, unfortunately, he will be to cowardly to do even that. This type is hard to read because he won't communicate any of this to you because he's too afraid of what you might think of him so you will have to try and figure it out on your own long after he's gone.

"Mr. Taken" may be taken with you but is unavailable because he is married or otherwise, in a serious relationship with someone else. He's bored at home and looking for a little excitement in his life. He will get you to feel sorry for him by telling you how bad he's got it with the wife and how she neglects his needs.

He will wine, dine and sixty-nine you until you're emotionally attached and then will either string you along with the promise that he's leaving her just as soon as the kids, who are now four and eight, turn eighteen. He can disappear suddenly when things look like they're getting too serious, you start making demands for more of his time, or his wife finds out.

"Slim Shady" will make you his lady and make you feel like you're the only girl in his world. He will tell you exactly what you want to hear, act like a perfect gentleman by opening doors for you, impress you with expensive gifts, and fancy dinners and make you feel secure as he talks about the future with you.

But, he has many dark secrets. When he's with you he appears perfectly normal. But, when you're not around, he's picking up one night stands, some may even be with a man.

He's good at covering his tracks and putting up a front yet, that can only last so long before his true colors start to surface. By then you've already moved in, become an emotional wreck, and wondering who this person is and how you can extricate yourself from the relationship.

"Mr. Mum" is a single dad who shares custody with his kids. If they're in middle school they will require a lot of his attention and you may be relegated to the back burner.

These types are capable of being in a serious relationship and sometimes, anxious to do so, but they will let you know that their kids come first, which is fine, if you don't mind not being the center of his world or have kids of your own.

This type of relationship is harder for single women who don't have kids. Dates may need to be broken at the last minute if his kids need him and he will have a lot of interaction with his ex-wife which may bother you, depending on the nature of that relationship.

If you decide to forge ahead with this type, you may suddenly be thrust into the role of step mum, a role you may not be prepared for especially if the children are young and having psychological and emotional problems due to their parents divorce.

They may even resent you or be disrespectful toward you because you took daddy away from mummie. Prepare yourself, and read all the books you can on parenting and dating a divorced dad.

"Mr. Moneybags" is the self made millionaire type who probably won't get involved with a woman over 40 unless he happens to be in his late fifties or early sixties. But, if by some chance, you happen to attract this type, you will congratulate yourself on your good fortune.

But beware. This type can be selfish because everything must go his way and he may even belittle you or criticize you simply because you haven't achieved all that he has.

This type usually prefers tall, leggy model types on their arm and may even instruct you on how to dress and wear your hair although, you looked perfectly fine to begin with. He will usually talk about himself a lot, not really interested in your point of view on things, can be vain and egotistical and disappointing or selfish lovers.

"The C Blocker" is the most dangerous type because you may or may not even be aware that he exists. He is the guy who secretly desires you and may find reasons to dislike you all at the same time but the part of him that has feelings for you won't have him making a move and approaching you himself.

He can be vindictive, nasty and angry at you for no apparent reason yet, he somehow finds willing participants to do his dirty work for him by lashing out at you and paying you back for absolutely nothing since you're not even a part of his life.

He will have a keen interest in you; will charm your friends so he can find out all he can about you, and may even flirt with or sleep with your so called girlfriends to feel closer to you in some weird way or for some perceived vindication.

They will of course, being the loyal girlfriends that they are NOT keep all of this from you. Whatever they share with him about you, will oftentimes, be information that he may use against you if he feels like you have wronged him in some way. Sadly, he doesn't care if his actions are causing you to suffer unnecessarily, that's his point. To see you suffer.

He will send guys your way that he thinks you may like, ones he can control and manipulate, get them to share intimate details about you with him then get them to dump you if he feels things are getting too serious. Surprisingly, these guys will back off quickly leaving you to wonder what happened.

"The C Blocker" has a guy code that let's other men know that you belong to him even though he may never make a move to claim you for himself. If you happen to meet someone he has no control over he will go out of his way to make you look bad by feeding your new guy lies and whatever else he can think of that may persuade him to dump you just because he can't stand to see you happy with someone else.

He may even be in a relationship himself but will still do whatever it takes to block you from getting serious with anyone else just in case he finally decides to make his move or out of sheer spite.

This type will probably never make a move even if you happen to know who he is and have shown interest in him at some point. Your only hope is to find someone who will be man enough to stand up against him and won't allow himself to be easily influenced or manipulated by him, will see your potential and consider you such a catch that he will basically tell him, "so sorry, your loss, she's mine!"

Now that you've had a refresher course on what types to avoid not only will you recognize them before ever getting involved with these types in the future you can focus your energy and attention on attracting the guy who won't have hang-ups about your flaws or care about your age and will make you the center of his world.

He will love you just the way you are and the relationship won't seem like a job where you're left guessing how to please this man whose only real interest is himself.

Step 11:

What Types Of Men Have You Been Drawn To In The Past?

Why do you think you have been drawn to these types? What steps can you take if you meet this type again in the future to protect yourself from hurt, pain and disappointment?

Chapter Twelve
How To Attract Mr. Right

Have you ever wondered why you attract the types of men that you do? Are you more concerned with being in love than being with the type of person whose core values and principles match your own?

We're all guilty, at one time or another, of choosing men who we know are just not right for us. But, in our hearts, we believe he can change or we can work on changing him into what we want him to be.

Even if we succeed in molding and reshaping this man, he will resent us for it later. We would cease to be the alluring, sexual creature that he fell in love with and his interest in us would probably diminish. And, in the end, we could lose him anyway.

We talked about a few of the standout types to avoid in the last chapter. But how do you go about attracting the right type if you've always been drawn to the wrong type?

The first thing you must do is gain more self-confidence in yourself. You may think you're a confident woman and I"m not saying you're not. But, confident women don't believe there is a man shortage nor are they afraid of not finding someone more suitable, knowing deep down, that they are staring Mr. Wrong in the face and need to walk away.

A confident woman doesn't go after another woman's man either. If Mr. Wrong tells you he is married or otherwise taken, but would still love to see you because he can't help being attracted to you, thank him, tell him you're flattered, but do yourself a favor and walk away. It won't end favorably.

Some women actually enjoy the attention and excitement an otherwise unavailable man provides as you contemplate the exciting, sexual relationship the two of you will be engaging in. But, then what? Is it worth becoming emotionally attached only to see him drive away and back into the arms of his wife?

Now you've not only closed yourself off from possibly meeting the right guy you have consciously or subconsciously taken yourself off the market so you can be available when he wants to see you.

This doesn't sound like it will be a confidence booster when you are considered "the other woman" or sloppy seconds. Your confidence will actually start to diminish as you get fidgety and anxious when you don't see him because he has family obligations that come first.

And, if by some chance, he decides to leave his wife or current girlfriend for you then you have to live on the edge wondering if he will cheat on you with someone else since that seems to be a part of his nature.

If you're consistently drawn to unavailable men then ask yourself why? Our personalities are made up of unique character traits that draw certain types of people to us whether they are friends are members of the opposite sex.

It can be a complex and frustrating experience if you spend too much time dwelling on the algorithms of a perfect match. There are no perfect matches. You will have to give and take and figure out what you will and won't tolerate in a new relationship. And, a man who is unavailable to you and involved with someone else should not be considered relationship material.

I am definitely ready to start dating again but I'm not looking for casual dating so therefore, I am being more selective in the type of men that I will actually make time for since my time is precious and limited.

On my priority list of what qualities a man must possess is taking care of himself and having pride in his body. He doesn't have to be a model type or have six pack abs or be a body builder.

But he certainly needs to be health conscious and make eating right and exercising a priority because I hold myself to that same standard. If he is negligent with his own needs then how will he be sensitive and caring about mine?

We all have a certain type in mind that we are physically attracted. However, we should consider broadening our approach and being open minded to other types that might spark an attraction and that meet our core requirements.

You can tell right away if you're attracted to someone but the real challenge is getting to know him as a person and learning all you can about his character traits, what he likes to do for fun, his personality and what his values are and if those values will mesh with your own.

If you're active and love being on the go, going away on weekends and exploring new locales, you are not going to be happy with a couch potato who enjoys lounging all weekend, drinking beer and watching reruns.

If you enjoy a certain level of sophistication and love talking about the finer things of life and being surrounded by elegant, well rounded people, you may be unhappy with the guy who has never left his hometown, has never owned a passport and thinks an exotic locale is his small hometown.

I'm not saying opposites can't attract nor should you look for a male clone of yourself or dive back in with Mr. Wrong because it feels comfortable and familiar. Just be open to new types of men and experiences that you think you may find enjoyable and give it a shot.

You don't need to have everything in common or be joined at the hip once you do get into another relationship. It's good to have your own hobbies and activities that you like to do apart from him.

It makes for a much better relationship and gives each the space needed. You want him to be not only your best friend whom you trust but also your most incredible lover.

Finding Mr. Right will mean avoiding all the places that you know Mr. Wrong types probably hang out such as bars and clubs. Some of you may be disagreeing saying, "what's wrong with bars and clubs?" Ask yourself what's right about them?

I think 40 and 50 year olds still clubbing hoping to meet someone, in that environment, looks kind of desperate and pathetic. If it didn't work out in your twenties, then honestly, it isn't going to work out today. Unless you're celebrating a girls night out or bachelorette party I would avoid these places if you're serious about meeting someone that you consider dating material.

Meeting men in a more suitable environment and having the confidence to go it alone or with one other girlfriend in tow will make you much more approachable than being part of a larger group of girlfriends.

And, please don't make the expensive mistake I made several years ago by hiring an expensive dating service to find your dream mate. Perhaps this may have worked out for a lucky few but, for me, it was a disaster.

The service cost almost $5,000. I was interviewed for over three hours to determine who I might be compatible with and what physical characteristics were important to me. I had to set up monthly payment arrangements since I couldn't afford to pay this hefty sum up front. It turned out not to be worth the expense.

My first date happened to be set up on Valentine's Day with a guy from Sweden. He was a scientist, introverted and boring. I had to keep the conversation going although he did ask me questions about growing up in Germany. At the end of the date he asked if he could borrow some cash to pay for his parking! That was the first and last date with him.

The 2nd date was supposed to be set up with a divorced father of two who happened to work out at my gym but I wasn't sure who he was. Once we connected on the phone I learned that he was not divorced and still living in the same house as his wife. Apparently, things were getting very ugly and they were fighting over finances and the kids.

I had been informed by the agency that the members had to be single and out of the home they shared with their former partner. But this was not the case with this guy. I ended up not even going out on a date with him because I didn't want to be involved in his family drama. And, he certainly wasn't ready for a relationship.

It went downhill from there as I was potentially set up on dates with people I had no interest in meeting after talking to them on the phone and either not clicking or we just didn't have anything in common to talk about so it didn't make sense to waste their time or mine meeting in person. I realized this was not what I signed up for and cancelled my membership.

I was surprised that for the money I was putting out that I wasn't getting quality introductions. It took another month of phone calls to get them to stop drafting my bank account.

I ended up having to close the account altogether because they would conveniently forget to stop taking money out of my account every month. It turned out to be a stressful and costly mistake on my part. I learned that these forced introductions just didn't work, at least not for me.

However, there are other less costly ways to meet men without joining expensive matchmaking services. Simply, by making a list of things you might enjoy doing that you have not tried in the past can open the doors of opportunity to meet others.

Even if you don't find the man of your dreams you can always make a new friend or use that time to network. I always enjoyed playing miniature golf so decided to join a Meet up group that included golf lessons with a golf pro. I figured I would give the real thing a try and meet some new people in the process.

I didn't attend with any expectations except to learn the game and be outside on a beautiful course. I met some wonderful people and although, I didn't see any potential dates, I enjoyed the company.

Keeping an open mind can open all sorts of doors to meeting men. Next, I was invited to a hockey game for a first date with a hockey player. Although, he turned out not to be someone I was interested in becoming serious with I did enjoy the game.

I noticed that the two teams had a few women playing hockey and admired these women for taking on a sport dominated by men. But what better way to meet someone!

As women, we have to think outside the box when it comes to where men frequent that could be potential dates. You probably won't find them hanging out at women's shopping centers unless they are shopping with or for their wives.

Think sporting events, tailgate parties, seminars, conferences, volunteer organizations, such as, Habitat For Humanity and trade shows oriented toward a specialty that men would frequent.

If this all sounds like too much work and you just want to give the online thing a try I suggest going to your site of choice and doing a search of men you are physically attracted to.

Next, go through their profile carefully looking at photos and reading everything that they have posted about themselves. If you have gone through the personal development exercises and have a clearer picture of the types of men you need to avoid you will start to notice things about their online profile that could be warning signs for you to stay away from that type.

I recently received a "wink" from a guy that resembled my ex boyfriend. His photo showed him shirtless and wearing board shorts with dark wrap around sunglasses. He had a very nice physique, at least in his main picture.

He also had facial stubble which I find sexy on some men and a nice tan. Even though I had cancelled my membership I was intrigued and wanted to check out his profile and other pictures.

Because I didn't allow myself to drool over his main photo and decided to look at his profile objectively I was able to determine that the main profile photo was not even recent because he posted other photos that were dated and only photographed from the neck up. That meant he was hiding something about his body. His face was puffier in these pictures and he didn't look like he was taking good of care of himself.

This was probably due to all the garbage he ate at the fast food joints he listed as favorite places to eat. He said he loved going to sports bars and drinking with his buddies. He was 38, the same age my ex boyfriend was when I met him. He was ex-military which was a plus, but didn't mention what type of work he was doing now for a living.

I started to feel uneasy as I continued reading his profile as there were a few similarities to my ex. My intuition was telling me to pass and not wink back or contact him. He did eventually try to make contact with me again but I didn't respond.

Attracting men isn't the problem for many of us. It's the types of men we attract. We lose our heads and give away our hearts way to quickly when we meet a guy. We need to slow down, take our time and enjoy the ride.

Don't start fantasizing that he must be the ONE when you meet him and start planning your wedding in your head. This is the time to think logically and not be swayed by emotions. Give yourself time to get to know him and figure out if this is indeed the right one. And, listen to that inner voice or intuition.

Of course, you don't want to come across as standoffish or cold and bitter. If you still harbor these types of feelings then you are not ready for a new relationship and that's fine. Give yourself more time. Honestly, what's the rush?

If you are ready to start dating again keep an open mind while guarding your heart. As a confident, self assured woman who knows what is best for her you will not settle for less nor will you allow yourself to be drawn to men who will end up hurting you again.

Write out an oath that states you will walk away from a relationship that's not right for you or feels like a repeat of a past failed relationship. As an empowered woman you can walk away, not with a sense of fear wondering if you will find somebody else, but with faith, knowing that it's already happened. You're just waiting to meet him.

Step 12:

A promise to my other self.

Oath of Faith

I _____ promise to walk away from any relationship that isn't right for me. I will listen to my inner voice and intuition and not be swayed by good looks alone. I will not allow myself to be consumed by this person and will continue to love myself, work on my personal development, pursue my dreams and learn new life skills. I will not spend time analyzing him or filling in the blanks with my own theories and reasonings. I will use my best judgement and pray for discernment and understanding.

Signed:_____ Date_____

Chapter Thirteen
Warning Signs You Should Never Ignore

Let's be clear we will never find a good guy if we keep chasing the bad guys. Good guys are boring and predictable, right? Bad guys are unpredictable and keep us guessing about everything from how they really feel to where they were last night when they couldn't be reached and didn't return any of our phone calls or text messages until the next day.

There are always excuses such as he didn't hear his phone ringing or somehow didn't receive the text. Some men are really good at lying and we know they're lying but overlook their lies because they are so good at making it up to us.

We say we want good guys who will treat us with respect and be faithful and dedicated to the relationship. But, why do we allow ourselves to consistently be drawn to the bad boy types?

To find the answers requires some real soul searching. When we allow men to treat us badly we are subconsciously telling ourselves that we don't deserve better. It's not ok for a guy to be abusive, physically nor mentally. We have to be aware of the signs before we get deeply involved and be prepared to walk away.

By changing our thought patterns and the way we view ourselves and others we can break this vicious and destructive cycle. Most people don't like working on themselves or trying to improve because its exactly that, "work". They would rather be comfortably numb in their dysfunctional state than think about what's wrong with them.

When we finally do meet a guy and realize he isn't the one our intuition alerts us that something isn't right about this person. But we brush those feelings aside. Maybe we haven't been with someone in a long time and are tired of waiting so why not have a bit of fun?

Should you decide to get involved with this person, no matter how hot he is, think about where this is leading? The guy that wants to invest time in you, taking you out to dinner and on weekly dates and showing genuine interest by pursuing you at a nice pace, not rushing you into anything and respecting your wish not to get intimate too quickly is probably on the right track.

Even a good guy will push to see how far you will allow him to go so it's up to you to slow things down a bit. The guy who runs hot and cold and then comes on strong with sweet words and then talks about spending his life with you all within a few weeks of meeting you is probably not being sincere and you should proceed with caution.

I met a guy online a couple of years ago that lived in Orlando and we seemed evenly matched. We had great conversations on the phone and kept the lines of communication open.

This guy had yet to meet me but was already talking about our future together. He sensed my skepticism especially after I told him that I had met guys before that had come on strong quickly and the relationship would fizzle just as fast.

He didn't miss a beat as he promptly informed me that he wasn't my past, but my present and my future. He was so convincing that I actually believed him and was on cloud nine for a while until it was time for us to finally meet in person. He ended up canceling our date, supposedly, because of job obligations and shortly thereafter, stopped calling altogether.

I had not even met this guy but had allowed myself to get emotionally involved and be seduced by his words. I may have met him and decided I wasn't even attracted to him. He might have lied and not even been the person in the photos he had posted online. He may have been married or in a relationship. Who knows. But none of that crossed my mind at the time. It was his words that had seduced me completely and left me upset and disillusioned.

You don't even have to sleep with a guy for him to have your head spinning if you allow emotions to rule your head and your heart. Although, we don't want to walk into a new situation with a suspicious attitude or a chip on our shoulder we need to control our emotions until we really get to know a person.

Guys have a way of coming on strong in the beginning, saying and doing all the right things, and may spend some time sweeping us off our feet so it's easy to fall for that and believe that this is the real thing when it's happening.

Some of these men should have won Academy Awards for their performances. They come across like perfect gentlemen in the beginning of a relationship. They hold the door for us to enter first, say all the right things, are thoughtful and considerate and very affectionate, kissing all the time and holding hands.

By the time the relationship starts to get serious and we move in together and then settle into a normal routine things start to change dramatically. They no longer hold the door open for us, start shutting us out, stop communicating and show very little affection or none at all. We sit and wonder, "who is this person I'm living with?" And, "what happened to the sweet, exciting guy I met and fell in love with?"

I know my ex-boyfriend did all of the above in the beginning. But a year later he was almost like a complete stranger. He didn't hold doors open for me any longer and he stopped being affectionate except for maybe a quick peck on the lips.

He would no longer hold my hand in public, as he had done in the beginning of our relationship and started walking three steps ahead of me, as if we weren't even together, so he could check out other women. It didn't matter if they were younger or older as long as they were not me.

Then he bought a new luxury SUV that I had picked out for him and it had a white interior so every time I got into his vehicle he snapped at me not to get my makeup on anything and why did I have to wear that stuff in his vehicle. He had always loved and appreciated how I fixed myself up, in the beginning, and then he later complained bitterly about it.

He used to sit next to me and cuddle on the couch while watching TV together. That turned into him sitting on the other side of the living room on the couch and surfing the web on his phone the entire evening while he ignored me sitting on the opposite side on the love seat.

If I complained he would get angry and say I was never satisfied. He came home every night and shut me out, but he was there, sitting on the opposite side of the room and considered this spending quality time together.

If I decided to join him on the couch and lean into him to give him a kiss or show him affection he would get uneasy and tell me to go back over to my side of the room. It was a humiliating experience.

On the rare occasions that we were intimate it was always rushed and I felt he was just going through the motions as he appeared detached and unemotional. Our relationship was still too new to have settled so quickly into such a boring routine but any suggestions I made to liven things up were ignored.

I knew he still found me attractive because he would come over and grab me or when it was just the two of us out on the boat he would take pictures of me in my bikini when he thought I wasn't looking. His behavior was bizarre and strange.

The guy who had swept me off my feet and was so sensual and romantic in the beginning was gone. I didn't know or recognize this person that I was in a relationship with any longer and it was disheartening.

I believe some guys love the newness and excitement a new relationship brings. But once the newness and the excitement have worn off they no longer appear interested and start looking outside the home for their next conquest. They have already conquered us so they don't feel the need to try any longer or work on the relationship to keep the romance alive.

These types of men are sometimes hard to discern in the beginning stages of a relationship because they do appear genuine and sincere. But one thing I learned is that they will reveal things about past relationships that are clear warning signs to walk away.

If he has been through a string of relationships that didn't last longer than a few months or a year or two this could mean he has long term commitment issues. If he refuses to even talk about his past or abruptly changes the subject that could be a warning sign that this person may not be ready for a relationship. He may have problems opening up so communication will always be an issue or he may be hiding something.

Please don't think that once you get into a relationship with this person that you will change him or that he will be different with you. Men are not supposed to be our pet project.

And, if you're already making a mental list of what needs to be changed either with his personality or physically then maybe he isn't the right guy for you and you've just made the decision to settle for someone who truly isn't your type.

The other thing some men will do if they sense you pulling back is they step it up another notch and come on even stronger. I had nagging doubts about giving up my life on the East Coast to move to the Midwest and had voiced my concerns to Chris.

He would text me in the middle of the night or call me saying he couldn't sleep because he needed me so much and that he would feel much better once I was there laying next to him every night.

Of course I fell for that even when the uneasy feelings were still there in the back of my mind telling me not to do this. Once I actually moved into his home I figured out why he was so uneasy and couldn't sleep and, in my opinion, those reasons had nothing to do with his undying love and devotion for me.

As women, our intuition is pretty strong. Yet, we ignore it when we should be examining why we are feeling this uneasiness that just won't go away. I believe it is God's way of subtly telling us that we are making the wrong decision.

Now is not the time to derail all that you worked so hard for in your spiritual and personal growth. Sometimes, we can feel vulnerable and make ourselves believe that there is no harm in getting to know this person we seem to have a connection with and before you know it we are hooked.

We just want to have a little fun and let go and be carefree. But, trust me, the fun will be at your expense not the hot eye candy that is slowly seducing you with his words. I urge you not to make the same mistakes over and over again. Choose wisely and give yourself time to really get to know someone you intend to spend your life with.

Men have a way of remaining emotionally detached and can look you straight in the face and lie and tell you whatever they think you want to hear. And they can do it so convincingly that we believe them and take them at their word.

We may think this won't happen again to us but if we look back over our past history with men we may notice a pattern of attracting the wrong types that are not good for us. The question is, if Mr. Wrong comes calling will we be able to escape his seductive words and think clearly and logically and walk away if necessary?

Sometimes when we get tired of waiting we push forward into a disastrous situation with anyone we find attractive. We see strangers walking down the street holding hands, friends getting married, maybe even an ex gets engaged or enters quickly into another relationship with another woman and we wonder why we are still single and start to panic that we haven't found anyone yet.

We learn by trial and error but we certainly don't want to spend the rest of lives paying for mistakes that could have been avoided had we quieted our minds and listened to God's voice instead of our own.

Step 13:

What warning signs do you need to be more aware of when you first start dating someone new?

Looking back at your past relationships what were the warning signs that showed you that relationship was probably not going to work out? Why do you think you chose to ignore your intuition and proceeded anyway?

Chapter Fourteen
Turning Lust Into Love

What's the difference between lust and love? This is the question posed to Antonio Banderas's movie character in the movie, Original Sin. "Love, you want to give and give more. Lust, you want to take and take more, devour, consume."

Some people have fallen in love at first sight while others have taken their time getting to know each other taking it slow and steady. Still others, having been badly burned avoid falling in love at all costs and will even end a relationship for no reason. Others may make it clear they are not looking for anything serious because of the emotional involvement.

But the way couples look at each other especially in the beginning stages of a relationship, the subtle nuances in a touch, the way you kiss and even specific words or phrases you use exclusively for each other can be the driving force behind that barely contained desire.

It's the power of words and the deep impact they can have creating that burning flame that can't be easily extinguished. Can you remember a time when you fell in love and your significant other spoke the words, "I love you", first?

It was probably the greatest feeling in the world. Or, a time, when you first got engaged and your significant other asked you to marry him. It probably took your breath away.

We all get to that point in a relationship where we can't keep our hands off of each other, where we are mesmerized by one another and intoxicated by each other's words and nuances. But, if you want this romance and passion to build into something deeper and lasting you really have to take it slow.

I've had to many conversations with friends who gave themselves away to quickly sometimes on the same night or within a week or two of meeting a guy and usually, within the month, he was already pulling away. Why? Because you gave him what he wanted way to quickly. This shouldn't be a surprise, by now, to most of us. Yet, women still fall into this trap.

When we were in our twenties we probably didn't put much thought into taking things slow or even thinking of a long term commitment, although, for me, I was already married in my early twenties so I didn't experience lots of boys and dating.

When we reach our forties we have probably had enough experiences and learned enough lessons to realize what works for us personally and what doesn't. Yet, I think some women get into a relationship and forget what they learned and how they were burned and end up repeating the same vicious cycle.

If you want to turn lust into love then this is what you are going to have to do. Earn each other's trust. Don't lose your head and common sense by just giving the goods away on the first, second or third date. Of course, there are no fast and hard rules that need to be followed, and every situation is different but you should really get to know each other first.

What are his likes and dislikes? Are you compatible? What does he like to do for fun? Does your lifestyle mesh with his? What were his past relationships like and why is he single now? You need to find out as much as you can about this person (without drilling him of course) but in a natural gradual way.

You probably won't get all the answers on the first, second or even third date. Getting to know each other takes time and doesn't happen overnight. That's why it's so important not to sleep with someone right away.

When you're trying to establish a relationship you only have a vague idea of who this person is based on what he has told you. Let him show you, overtime, who he is. This is the only way to get to know someone.

In a relationship, you won't be in the lust stage forever and if you hope to spend your life with this person then it's imperative that you get to know as much as you can about each other's values and what each of you need and want out of a relationship. Trust me, within the first year of dating a guy already knows if he wants to spend his life with you even if he doesn't come out and tell you this.

I love the expectancy a new relationship brings; holding hands, the looks of desire for each other, kissing all the time, the way you touch and caress each other and the time spent just getting to know each other and learning something new about the other that makes two complete strangers come together and blossom into a relationship.

But as that relationship flourishes the lustful stage brings out very strong emotions that are hard to tame. You must find a way not to lose your head during this process. There is nothing sexy about sex before monogamy if you want that lustful stage to grow into something deeper where you are both falling in love with each other.

So, how do you get to that stage of falling in love? By staying out of the bedroom. If you're spending all of your time together making out and not going out you're going to have a disconnect between the two of you when you're not in bed.

By getting to know each other first you can get a clearer understanding of where the relationship is going. Go out on dates and see how you interact in public with each other. Are you compatible? Is he a fun date? Or a bore? Is he affectionate in public? Does he hold your hand? Again, you won't find these things out behind closed doors.

And, if he doesn't want to talk about himself, changes the subject or tries to seduce you and then says, "we can talk about all those things later," take that as a warning sign that this guy is either not taking you seriously or hiding something. You may need to back off completely if necessary until he learns to open up with you.

Don't get so wrapped up in your new relationship that you put your life on hold or give up on your dreams. It's very important to continue doing what you were doing before you met this person.

Continue to work on building that business you just started or pursuing your goals. I think men find a woman even more desirable when she's got her own thing going on and isn't sitting around waiting for her man to entertain her all the time. You also don't want to be with the guy who doesn't make time for you and isn't putting in the time required to grow your relationship into something deeper.

But before you met him you had a life so continue on that path. You're a busy woman which means he is going to have to work at pursuing you. And when you do get together don't spend that time telling him your entire life story or gossiping about your girlfriends.

Be subtle and reveal things about yourself in stages so he is always pleasantly surprised as he gets to know you. As you're getting to know each other don't bore him with long drawn out stories about a friend's cheating husband or about family members you don't get along with.

Share important and relevant information about yourself without overwhelming him with your life story. And convey what you need to say without sounding long winded. Don't try to get everything in about yourself on the first couple of dates.

Allowing yourself to open up by saying the right thing, at the right time, in the right way, to the right person will allow you to be authentic and transparent.

In this way you draw the person in by showing them your strengths but also letting them see a bit of your weaknesses and faults so that they can better relate to you as a person and hopefully, be willing to do the same. This is how you begin to shape your relationship.

Once you have gotten to that stage of dating exclusively and you feel comfortable with each other plan a romantic weekend get-away. Let your first time together be special where there won't be any distractions and you can focus your attention on having a pleasurable and intimate experience.

After making him pursue you and not giving in so easily he will be all to eager to go away with you. You will appreciate having waited even during those times where you desperately wanted to give in.

One thing you don't want to do, and it still amazes me that adults in their forties and beyond still do this, is play games with each other. I urge you not to lead him on, ignore his text messages for hours or cancel dates at the last minute as some type of ploy. This can backfire real fast and doesn't make for the start of a promising relationship.

If you want that lust to turn into a deep abiding love then take it slow, put your past behind you and let him see you as the self confident, empowered woman who is capable of expressing love.

Sometimes when a relationship is moving along at a nice pace some guys will start to get cold feet and back off because their feelings are scaring them and they don't know how to handle these incredibly strong emotions they are feeling for you.

They think because they are men they aren't supposed to fall this hard for a woman and are afraid of losing themselves with you. If you notice this happening don't make assumptions. You need to talk about this in a non-threatening, non-accusing way and see if he will open up to you about it.

If he doesn't, continue to do your thing and let this be his problem not yours. If he continues in this way he will end up losing you altogether to someone else and it will be his loss.

As the relationship progresses it should get better and grow stronger. Your love for one another should grow deeper. Your love life should become even more intense, exciting even and you shouldn't be afraid to show affection toward one another in public. He should be the rock you can lean on and when one or the other is feeling down you should lift each other up.

And provided neither of you will allow your fears to hold you both back from progressing, and you're mature enough to get through the inevitable rough patches, there will come a day when you absolutely cannot live without each other and will want to spend the rest of your lives together.

Before you know it you will be thanking God that last relationship didn't work out because he has so much better in store for you this time around and you can finally say you have met the man of your sweet dreams.

Step 14:

What steps can you take to make sure you are not rushing into an intimate situation too quickly?

What must you do to slow the guy down who wants to take things way to fast? If you've taken things to far, to soon and hitting some bumps in the road with your new relationship how can you work together to turn things around?

Chapter Fifteen
The Secret To A Happy & Lifelong Relationship

With divorce at an all time high it's increasingly hard to find couples, in our generation, who are still happily married today. Many of us got married in our twenties and are now divorced. A few of my friends are on their second or third marriages.

Couples are much quicker to call it quits today than to work on the relationship and resolve issues quickly before they escalate. Usually, one or the other doesn't want to communicate what's bothering them and pretend that everything is fine while harboring old resentments.

Lack of communication is the death of any relationship. Unresolved conflict leads to anger, frustration and alienation. One should have the ability to feel safe opening up and discussing issues with each other without fear of being judged. Respect for each other's opinions, ideas, and feelings should be taken seriously.

Once you decide to become an exclusive couple you need to discuss what is important to you in that relationship. Don't get caught up in the ideal of being married while neglecting your plans and goals for the relationship itself. Ask the important questions about where you see yourselves, as a couple, in two years, five years, and so on.

Do you plan on buying a home? Opening a business together? Having children? Perhaps you both enjoy travel and want to see the world and will plan yearly trips to exotic locations. Do you plan on sharing everything with each other and having no boundaries? Or, do you feel like you need some boundaries in place to feel like you have your space and freedom? And, what about finances?

Finances are one of the biggest issues that couples fight over. How will you split household bills? Who will pay for what? Will you keep separate bank accounts and open a joint account for household expenses? Does the person who makes the most money pay more out of pocket expenses?

Don't assume that he will take care of everything while you keep all your money to go shopping every weekend unless he expressly states this to you. You both need to be on the same page and not start making assumptions that once you become "Mrs." that your husband's opinion no longer matters.

If you happen to meet and marry a man who believes it's his duty to take care of his wife and pay for all or the majority of the household expenses then, congratulations! However, make sure you're still generating your own income so you're not completely dependent on your husband.

In my last relationship, one of our biggest problems centered around finances. When I met Chris I was doing quite well financially and had a great paying job. I gave it all up for what I thought was love and lost. The career job and the exceptional income were gone.

By year two of our relationship I could barely make ends meet once we moved down to the Florida Keys. There just wasn't any professional industry there. And, commuting back and forth to Miami was well over four hours each day.

However, I took up the challenge because I was desperate to make a decent salary again. I was offered an incredible job as the Director Of Sales & Marketing for a Miami magazine called *Healthy Miami Magazine.*

The Publisher's were a husband and wife from South America and were wonderful people to work for. But driving an SUV and commuting four hours each day was eating away at my salary and reluctantly, I had to give up the position.

So I was, once again, forced to take an hourly job which I hadn't had to do since high school. Chris, on the other hand, started doing quite well for himself in the marine industry and started making the kind of money I was making when he first met me. Yet, he still expected me to pay half the bills as if I were still making the great salary I once made.

Even when I pleaded with him that I couldn't afford to pay half of everything and that he needed to pick up the slack for a while until I could find a way to make more money he refused and threatened to kick me to the curb or told me to get out and get three jobs if necessary.

One night we got into a huge fight about the household bills. He was feeling resentful that I couldn't afford to pay half the rent as I had been able to do in the past even though during that low point in my life I was only making $11 an hour. Once again, his solution was that I should get out and get a second job even though I was already working 40 plus hours per week.

I remember becoming very upset and getting in my car on a week night and driving down to Key West to look for additional work. I had already worked nine hours that day and was tired and mentally exhausted.

Before I left the house I put on a sexy dress and high heels and headed straight for the most popular strip club. I obviously wasn't thinking clearly. I sat in the car for half an hour before I even got the courage to go inside.

I was nervous as I approached the manager and asked if they were hiring. He looked at me for a long time before handing me an application. All around me I saw both men and a few women checking me out. I felt uncomfortable so I went and sat in my car while filling out the application.

I had several men trying to pick me up right there in the parking lot. I hurriedly filled out the application and took it back inside only to have the manager pull me to the side and tell me that he didn't feel like I belonged in that type of environment.

He thought I looked too vulnerable. Even after I told him I wasn't he said he believed me but I still had this look of innocence on my face that made him feel uneasy hiring me.

I was there to get a job as a cocktail waitress figuring I could make decent tips without actually stripping even though I had felt uncomfortable in that environment and it must have somehow shown on my face.

As I drove back home exhausted and worn out from my wasted trip to Key West I wondered how someone who was supposed to love and cherish me wouldn't support me in my time of need and cut me some slack especially when he could afford to do so financially. But he didn't feel that I was his responsibility even though he was supposedly the man of the house.

Once my savings were depleted and he saw that no high paying job was forthcoming anytime soon I felt as if I was of no use to him. And, because we were not engaged, I was of the opinion, that he didn't feel committed or obligated to help me out financially.

I ended up pawning the diamond promise ring he gave me at the beginning of our relationship to help pay some of the household bills that he had stubbornly refused to pay which were due for shut-off the very next day. I figured if he cared so little for me then it didn't matter what I did with the ring. I lied and told him my mother had sent me the money to pay the bills.

His promises from the past meant nothing now when he thought so little of me. I really learned my lesson to not ever move in with someone again unless we were engaged to be married and had a discussion beforehand about finances and who would take care of what in case one of us fell on hard times.

Love doesn't keep a record of wrongs and certainly doesn't keep track of who does more in the relationship than the other. This is where resentment rears its ugly head, during times when one ends up paying more than the other and feeling taken advantage of instead of feeling good that they are contributing to the household.

Couples who are generous with each other and don't keep a record of how much they are spending on one another make for a much better relationship. If you're with someone who shows signs of being stingy and cheap this behavior is only going to get worse as the relationship progresses.

If your guy is madly in love with you he will enjoy buying things for you. He will encourage you to pursue your dreams and not hesitate to tell everyone how proud of you he is when you accomplish your goals. He will take his role as the man of the house seriously and step up to the plate when his damsel is in distress.

If he sees you're unhappy in some way he will go out of his way to help resolve the issues and will have your back no matter what the circumstances. He will want to alleviate any fears you may have about any aspect of your relationship and be willing to openly discuss any concerns you may have.

You have to consider that this partnership will be a long term commitment. One that requires work and not something that you can just dispose of once you get tired of it, like a material possession. You have to care enough about each other to survive the difficult stages the relationship will encounter.

We live in a disposable society. When we get tired of our car or house or other material possessions we want to get rid of them and get something else because we feel they will make us happy. Sadly, relationships are being treated the same way.

We would rather divorce and start over with someone new than work out existing problems and issues within that current relationship. If we get tired of having sex with the same person, we look elsewhere to have an exciting and secretive affair with someone else.

It's a vicious cycle of never being satisfied and always looking to see if the grass is greener on the other side. But what you most often find is not greener grass but a septic tank. People like that are never satisfied with anyone or anything and live miserable lives because they look for people and things to make them happy.

When they feel they are not getting that, then they look elsewhere instead of talking through their fears and concerns with their partner and finding ways to be happy within themselves.

No relationship will ever be perfect. Even good relationships go through bad times but, its how you handle the bad days that make all the difference between a relationship that can last a lifetime or one that can easily be cast by the wayside.

As women, we like to lead with our heart and emotions. But, when it comes to a lifelong relationship, we need to include logic and sound reasoning, while being cautious and using discernment.

Make sure your relationship is compatible and that you enjoy doing the same things or are at least willing to compromise. You want to have shared values, a common world view, adventurous travels, religious or spiritual ties, genuine desire for each other and an incredible sex life.

In the beginning of the relationship there is the ideal of each other but as time progresses one or the other starts to become disillusioned and now the relationship becomes an ordeal and before long you're looking for a new deal.

Healthy relationships have to let go of people, places and things from the past that were unpleasant. You have to keep your family out of your personal problems that arise between you and your significant other. You now become a priority to each other. And, you certainly don't want to make each other feel left out in any way.

Healthy relationships let go of guilt, grief and grudges. You want to start your new life with a fresh start without trying to cover up past hurts or bandage up old wounds.

And in your new relationship you want him to be someone you can trust and confide your deepest fears and your most ardent desires. You need that delicate balance of having him as your best friend and also your most passionate lover.

To keep the relationship fresh and the passion alive for each other you need to not get too complacent or lazy. Don't just start letting yourself go now that you've got your man or acting like you're his mother, ordering him around like a child. I assure you this will become a turn off real fast.

Relationships tend to fall apart when one partner starts to drift away from the other. When one becomes so preoccupied with something or someone other than their spouse, and spends more time cultivating outside interests while neglecting the relationship which is no longer a priority, you can guess where that relationship is headed next.

If it's the man who is suddenly drifting away now the woman starts nagging and making him feel guilty and he shuts down and pulls even further away from her until the relationship falls completely apart. At this point it will take divine intervention to mend the broken pieces.

But if you're not on the same wave length spiritually and are mismatched in your values you will have very little chance of sustaining your relationship or even figuring out how to get back to where you once were in the beginning when you were so in love with one another.

If you've come this far in reading this book, have given some thought to what went wrong in your past relationship and what you want and need in a future relationship I'm sure you now have a clearer picture of the type of man you desire to spend your life with that isn't based purely on physical characteristics alone.

Don't give up on yourself or put yourself down or wonder how you will ever find someone else who can love you the way you deserve. Don't be afraid to open yourself up to receiving that person who will be your biggest fan and your greatest love.

Step 15:

How can you keep the passion alive once you settle down in a relationship?

What steps can you take to ensure the lines of communication remain open where you feel safe to discuss any issues or concerns you may have with each other?

Chapter Sixteen
Pursuing Your Dreams After 40

I've spoken to many single women over forty, who are, understandably, struggling financially and working dead end jobs that have no future. Many are sending out resumes and getting no response and believe this has something to do with their age.

A woman from my church had contacted me to talk about how this has been a huge problem for her. Dana has worked the same job for 25 years and wanted to make a career change.

She had fallen on hard times as a single mother of a twenty something year old son, who had moved out of the family home. She was struggling every month to get the mortgage paid and couldn't even afford basic cable or high speed internet connection.

She was looking for a roommate as she had a spare bedroom and bath to rent out to help pay the bills. She was irate on the phone as she explained how all the available jobs were going to the younger generation and that no one wanted to hire her because of her age. She was now in her late forties and seemed lost and out of sorts with the way things were done in terms of searching for a job today.

She wasn't social media savvy and didn't have a Facebook page. She talked incessantly and jumped from one subject to another. It was hard to interact or get a word in edgewise. When I inquired if she had any dreams or aspirations she finally got quiet for a moment and then said she had, a long time ago, but felt it was too late now to start over.

How many women are out there in their forties and beyond who feel the same way? This belief that their lives are over and that it's too late to pursue their dreams so they might as well settle and spend the rest of their lives working in a job they hate and dreaming of what could have been. I think the job market in itself is tough as all ages compete and go after the same jobs.

However, there are still some incredible companies out there that will allow you to work from home, have an open door policy and provide full health benefits. One of the best industries to work in is the travel industry. Look for companies voted, "One of the 50 Most Engaging Places To Work" and set your sights on getting your foot in the door.

If it's a job you want then you have to learn all there is to know about that industry or company and follow their guidelines for submitting job applications online and staying up on changes in social media. To stand out from all the other applicants you may have to get creative and think outside of the box.

What college grads lack in experience they make up for in enthusiasm, positive energy and they have a teachable spirit.

They are eager to learn new things and understand the importance of social media and how it pertains to business.

Both men and women over forty are considered set in their ways, stubborn, don't want to be told or taught anything new and are close minded. Not all of us are like this but this is what society perceives us to be.

If it's a job you're after then you must be open to learning new ideas. If you happen to get an interview and come across as close minded and think Facebook and Twitter is for teenagers and you don't have time for that nonsense and have no idea what Instagram or Pinterest are then don't expect to be called back for round two of the interview process.

Instead of expending negative energy and lamenting the ways of the world and making excuses about how unfair the job market is and how discriminatory companies are against hiring you because of your age then do something about it. Don't allow this to hold you back. If you don't give up and keep pressing forward you can find that dream job. They are out there and are open to hiring women in our age bracket.

There are many career options out there that are perfect for women over forty. What do you love to do? Go back to school and learn Interior Design. Get your Real Estate License and sell homes specializing in a specific niche market. Learn the travel industry and enjoy the perks of discounted or free trips to exotic destinations.

Even if you have a desire to write a book or conduct online workshops you can do this in your spare time after work like I did and still make progress by taking steps each day that will have you accomplishing those goals.

When you're single you have time on your hands in the evening and on the weekends. What better way than to use that time off from work constructively by learning new life skills or working on a hobby that can turn into a moneymaker.

When you keep yourself busy working on projects you enjoy you won't have time to feel sorry for yourself if you're home alone on a Saturday night. Think about how good you will feel once you've accomplished your creative goals.

And, when the day comes that you finally meet someone special your projects will be near completion or completed and you can feel good knowing that you are on the path to both career and financial success and can enjoy your new relationship without feeling stressed and burdened.

Since I started writing this book almost a year ago I also came up with the idea to create copywriting modules to help other women start their own freelance copywriting business based on their passions.

Copywriters are in demand especially in specialized niches such as the travel industry, health and wellness and many more. I show women how to effectively make use of the time they have off after work and on the weekends to accomplish their assignments since it's a program they can complete at their own pace.

By teaching women copywriting skills, helping them define their niche while creating a prosperity mindset plus providing them with marketing skills to grow their own freelance side business is a rewarding and exciting prospect for many.

And, all of this was done during nights and on weekends! I was determined to succeed and had nothing but time on my hands since I was't in a relationship and didn't want to spend that time focusing on being single and feeling sorry for myself.

One thing you don't want to do is compromise your day job. If it's a job that you love you certainly don't want to do anything to jeopardize your position. Don't use company time to work on personal projects. Give your current position your full attention during the day and use your lunch hour or evenings and weekends to do everything else.

Now, more than ever, is the perfect time to pursue your dreams and make them a reality. Otherwise, you will become frustrated and unhappy until you find a way to make it happen and get the motivation to put a plan into action.

Start small. But start somewhere. Don't allow another day to go by, don't make another excuse as to why you can't make it happen. Find a way to break down the barriers that have held you back for so long. You are the only one holding yourself back by your own fears and self doubt.

Unless you already have a thriving, successful business or a career that you love and are truly content, then cheers! You can definitely be an inspiration for other women who are trying to get on their feet and help advise them.

But for those who are hesitant to take that first step don't be content to accept mediocrity as your fate in life. Go out there and make a new life for yourself. You may be in the worst possible financial situation; unable to pay your bills and barely able to keep a roof over your head.

You may be stressed out and your mind wandering in fifty different directions at once. Take a breather and calm yourself down. It is during times of utter and complete chaos that I am reminded of what the Apostle Paul wrote in Philippians 4:12-13, "I know what it is to be in need, and I know what it is to have plenty.

I have learned the secret of being content in any and every situation, whether well fed or hungry, whether living in plenty or in want. I can do everything through him who gives me strength."

I was certainly going through my challenges in the past year and coming up against many obstacles yet I found a way to remain calm, centered and focused on what needed to be done so much so that a friend asked me if I was taking medication.

She couldn't believe that with everything I was going through, at the time, plus having the guy I was in love with for many years propose to someone else on Facebook, was just too much to bear.

Yet, even during my grief, and pain and loss I was somehow holding it all together and without medication. I believe everything happens for a reason or doesn't happen for a reason only known to God himself. Trust in him. He won't lead you astray.

I didn't need medication to alter my frame of mind and use it as a coping mechanism. Honestly, reading scripture and praying has been my medicine and I hope that when things get really tough for you that you will have faith and keep some scripture or quotes at hand that will center you and allow you to find some peace in the midst of all the chaos surrounding your life.

I continued writing and researching through my tears and pain to get my book completed. Sometimes I felt alone and alienated from family and what few friends that I had left that I could trust. But I refused to give up on my dreams of writing a book and becoming a published author.

I had tried so many other things that hadn't worked out because of lack of finances but didn't regret the journey I had taken to learn new things. At one point I had been an Esthetician with my own skincare studio, a Holistic Healthcare Practitioner, a professional singer/songwriter and a licensed Real Estate Agent. And, as a writer I can write a book about any one of these subjects or blog that could benefit someone else.

The beauty of life is that we can do so many different things. If we never try then we never have to worry about failing but we also never have to worry about succeeding either.

Bonus Steps:

Create a vision board of what your dreams may look like on paper or a virtual vision board.

For example, if you want to be an Interior Designer what types of homes do you want to design? For what type of people? Do you want to specialize or appeal to everyone?

Where do you see yourself living once your dreams start becoming a reality? And do you want your work featured in magazines? What about the cover of a magazine? Let your imagination run wild.

Put all of this and more on your board and look at it every day as a reminder of what you can accomplish especially during those times when you may become frustrated or hit a roadblock. And, if you're interested in starting your own freelance copywriting business visit my website www.inpraiseofsinglewomenover40.com.

Epilogue
This Is Not The End

This isn't the end of the story or the end of the road. No, this is your chance for new beginnings. If you're still single, you have many options out there to meet new and interesting people. You have only to get yourself out there and brush off any limiting beliefs or self doubts.

There is still so much for you to accomplish such as writing your own book or starting that business you've always wanted. Perhaps learning new life skills so you can switch or advance your career. Or, working in a dream job that allows you to work from home planning trips for your affluent client's to exotic locations.

No matter where you are in life and what battles you fought along the way, you can still achieve what you believe. We may carry battle scars from past broken relationships but they and the men who hurt us don't define who we are today and what we will become tomorrow.

We grow up dreaming of a world of possibilities. A dream job, dreamy husband and beautiful home with perhaps children and a dog. As little girls, we were read fairy tales about princesses being rescued by their prince or knight in shining armor.

As we get older we advance to romance novels, where the plot gets more complicated for the character and she faces many obstacles along the way, but in the end she gets the man of her dreams.

The problem with growing up reading these types of stories is that we grow up believing this is what we should receive in real life. Maybe some women have met their Prince Charming and are living the fairy tale life but for those of us who haven't, we don't have to wait for Prince Charming to create the life we've always wanted to live or sit around hoping to be rescued.

We can create that life on our own by taking small steps and adding one dream aspect at a time. We don't have to wallow in self-pity and bitter disappointment. We can grieve, then pick ourselves up and start over.

Life offers many chances to start again. The road doesn't have to be the road of broken dreams. The journey may be full of road blocks but we must find a way to go over, around or through them in order to succeed.

If we focus on the end result we may become overwhelmed, get discouraged, or fill our minds with negative self talk about how impossible it all seems. Take small steps each day, and before you know it, you will have achieved much more than you thought possible or realized.

We all want to meet our prince, and my wish is that we all do, but true satisfaction will come from creating the life you've always wanted to live and paving the way to making those dreams come true on your own.

It's time to re-write that happy ending to the fairytale. We don't need to be rescued by Prince Charming but we would love for him to be the one we ride off with into the sunset and spend the rest of our lives living happily ever after.

A Personal Invitation

This non fiction book involved real life situations which means the story has not come to an end. We each have our personal journey in life and there will be times when we're happy, times when we're sad and times when we face disappointments and setbacks.

But life is in constant motion and change is always eminent. As women in our forties and beyond we share a common bond that need not be broken on these pages.

Join me, or feel free to reach out to me through my online community at http://www.inpraiseofsinglewomenover40. com or follow me on twitter at http://twitter.com/overview40 or join the conversation on Facebook at http://Facebook.com/ inpraiseofsinglewomenover40.

Notes/Credits

Introduction

p. 1, Norine Dworkin McDaniel, *Happily Married? It's Good For Your Health*

Life Script, Women's Health Center, February, 2014.

p. 2, National Archive of Criminal Justice Data's Survey, Norine Dworkin McDaniel, *Happily Married? It's Good For Your Health*, Life Script, February 2014.

p. 10, The US Census Bureau, 2010.

Chapter One

p. 15, Elizabeth Wurtzel, *Elizabeth Wurtzel Confronts Her One Night Stand of a Life*, New York Magazine, January 14, 2013.

p. 19–20, Joel Osteen, *Become A Better You*, (New York: Free Press, A Division of Simon & Schuster, Inc., 2007).

p 20, See Ecclesiastes 11:4.

Chapter Two

p. 23, See "The Marriage Crunch," *Newsweek*, June 2nd, 1986.

p. 23, See Ecclesiastes 4:9; 4:10; 4:12.

Chapter Three

No special notes or resources quoted.

Chapter Four

No special notes or resources quoted.

Chapter Five

p. 53–54, See Colossians 3:13-14.

p. 54, Dr. John C. Maxwell, Christ Fellowship Notes from Sunday Service, 2011.

Chapter Six

No special notes or resources quoted.

Chapter Seven

p. 63, Joyce Meyer, *Battlefield Of The Mind*, (Faithwords, Hatchette Book Group, New York, NY, 1995, 2nd edition e-book, 2011).

p. 64, See *Pride & Prejudice*, Feature Film, (Universal Studios, 2007), Adapted from Jane Austen's Novel by same name originally published in 1813 by T. Egerton, Whitehall.

p. 67, Dr. John C. Maxwell, Christ Fellowship Notes from Sunday Service, 2011.

p. 67, See Philippians 4:8.

Chapter Eight

p. 74, Joyce Meyer, *Battlefield Of The Mind*, (FaithWords, Hatchette Book Group, New York, NY 1995, 2nd edition ebook, 2011).

Chapter Nine

p. 89, Morgan Spurlock, *Supersize Me,* (Documentary, Independent Filmmaker, 2004).

p. 89, *Jesus Of Nazareth*, (A Franco Zeffirelli Production, 1977).

Chapter Ten

No special notes or resources quoted.

Chapter Eleven

No special notes or resources quoted.

Chapter Twelve

No special notes or resources quoted.

Chapter Thirteen

No special notes or resources quoted.

Chapter Fourteen

p. 141, *Original Sin,* (Metro-Goldwyn Mayer Pictures, Inc., 2000).

Chapter Fifteen

p. 151, *Healthy Valley Miami* (Healthy Magazine, 2012-2013).

Chapter Sixteen

p. 164, See Philippians 4:12-13.

Lightning Source UK Ltd.
Milton Keynes UK
UKHW02f1211160618
324256UK00007B/266/P